Rosie Young

Rosie Young

A Lifetime of Selfless Service

Moira M. W. Chan-Yeung

Hong Kong University Press
The University of Hong Kong
Pok Fu Lam Road
Hong Kong
https://hkupress.hku.hk

© 2024 Hong Kong University Press

ISBN 978-988-8805-78-5 (*Hardback*)

All rights reserved. No portion of this publication may be reproduced or transmitted in any form or by any means, electronic or mechanical, including photocopying, recording, or any information storage or retrieval system, without prior permission in writing from the publisher.

British Library Cataloguing-in-Publication Data
A catalogue record for this book is available from the British Library.

Cover image: Professor Rosie Young passing the torch, at the homecoming dinner in celebration of the 130th anniversary of HKU Faculty of Medicine, 2017. Courtesy of the Faculty of Medicine, University of Hong Kong.

Digitally printed

Contents

Foreword by Professor Chak-sing Lau	vi
Preface	ix
Acknowledgements	xiii
Author's Note	xiv

Part 1

Chapter 1. Childhood	3
Chapter 2. Student Days	26
Chapter 3. An Academic in Medicine	51

Part 2

Chapter 4. Blazing a Trail: University Administrator	75
Chapter 5. A True Holistic Approach: Public Service in Medicine	93
Chapter 6. Mentor to Leader: Public Service in Education	118
Conclusion	138
Appendix 1: Curriculum Vitae of Rosie Young	143
Appendix 2: Publications of Professor Young Tse Tse, Rosie	148
Bibliography	158
Index	165

Foreword

Professor Rosie Young is such an inspirational figure to all of us in medicine and the wider community in Hong Kong and beyond that I commend Professor Moira Chan for putting together her life story in this monograph, the draft of which was my faithful companion on my first long-haul travel abroad following the three-plus year-long COVID-19 pandemic. In the same way that we learn from managing the pandemic—that we need to be vigilant, astute, persistent while flexible, and work as a team—the story of Professor Young teaches us to be inquisitive, perseverant, selfless, loyal, and collegial in becoming a clinician, teacher, researcher, and an administrator.

Hong Kong must be eternally grateful to Professor Young, who has dedicated her whole life to serving the city that she loves so much. During her illustrious career, Professor Young has touched the lives of countless people. Many of her students have gone on to become leaders in medicine, serving the community with compassion, knowledge, skill, and humility. Her patients leave her consultation room with their mind at ease and their anxiety relieved, knowing that they are in the best of hands. The politicians who have had the good fortune to receive shrewd advice from her have used it judiciously in bringing about policies that have helped to improve the health care of our citizens. And within the University of Hong Kong, everyone knows they can always count on Professor Young, as she is such a staunch supporter of her alma mater. Indeed, I have to personally thank Professor Young, for if it was not for her referral of me to Professor T. K. Chan back in 1991 when I was at a crossroads in my academic career, I would not have had the opportunity to return to Hong Kong and imitate her dedication to serving the university in the past three decades.

Professor Young's devotion to medicine and her patients never fails to amaze me. At the time of writing, Professor Young, who is ninety-two years young, still comes into her office every day to see patients and teach students in the clinics. She stays abreast of the latest advances in not only her own discipline, endocrinology, but generally everything else in general medicine. She is the most regular attendee of the Department of Medicine's weekly Grand Round and annual Medical Forum and never fails to stay the course of these meetings!

Professor Moira Chan, our famed medical historian cum professor of medicine, is similarly energetic, expending such enormous time researching the history of medicine in Hong Kong after her retirement. Her herculean effort has culminated in her previous publications of *A Medical History of Hong Kong* series of three books and this latest biography of Professor Young. Like her previous publications, this new addition is also resource-rich and includes not just the history of medicine in Hong Kong but also that of the city in the last one hundred years. Professor Chan's vibrant depiction of the life of this petite giant in medicine—the one and only Professor Rosie Young—makes this book a must read for all.

To reciprocate our love and respect for Professor Rosie Young, I would like to dedicate the following poem by Robert Burns (1759–1796),[1] the celebrated 'national poet' of Scotland, a country where Professor Young has such fond memories.

> *O my Luve's like a red, red rose,*
> *That's newly sprung in June;*
> *O my Luve's like the melodie*
> *That's sweetly play'd in tune.*

---

1. Scottish Poetry Library, https://www.scottishpoetrylibrary.org.uk/poem/red-red-rose/.

A fair art thou, my bonnie lass,
So deep in luve am I;
And I will luve thee still, my Dear,
Till a' the seas gang dry.

Till a' the seas gang dry, my Dear,
And the rocks melt wi' the sun:
I will luve thee still, my Dear,
While the sands o'life shall run.

And fare thee weel, my only Luve!
And fare thee weel, a while!
And I will come again, my Luve,
Tho' it were ten thousand mile!

Professor Chak-sing Lau, MBBS, JP
Dean of Medicine
Chair and Daniel C. K. Yu Professor in Rheumatology and Clinical Immunology
The University of Hong Kong

Preface

Professor Young Tse Tse Rosie is an accomplished doctor, a distinguished academic, and a highly respected public figure in Hong Kong. Born in the city in 1930, where she received her education, she completed her postgraduate training in the United Kingdom. On returning after her professional examination to become a specialist in internal medicine in 1960, she served her alma mater, the University of Hong Kong, and the community in Hong Kong, with great devotion, even up to now at the grand old age of ninety-two.

In 1954, she was appointed after internship as a clinical assistant at the Department of Medicine, the University of Hong Kong (HKU). She was promoted through the ranks to a personal chair professor in 1974. She established the first endocrinology and metabolic diseases unit, which became the clinical and research centre in Hong Kong, training all the sub-specialists in that discipline in the following two to three decades. Despite the heavy teaching and clinical duties, she managed to conduct relevant research until heavy administrative duties and public service work made it impossible for her to continue with research and clinical duties. Her talent for administration as sub-dean and then dean of the Faculty of Medicine was recognized by Vice-Chancellor Rayson Huang, who appointed her to be one of the two pro-vice-chancellors in 1985, a position which she held until 1993. When Vice-Chancellor Wang Gungwu retired in 1995, she declined the offer of being considered for the interim vice-chancellorship, which might eventually lead to appointment as vice-chancellor. She agreed to serve as acting pro-vice-chancellor for another year in 1996, and later as acting dean of students for two years before her official retirement from HKU in 1999.

As sub-dean of the Faculty of Medicine, she became a member of the Medical Council in 1978. However, her major contributions to public service in medicine began after she was elected chairman of the Medical Council in 1988. As chairman of the council, she championed reforms of the council and was responsible for implementing the Medical Registration (Amendment) Bill of 1995 to have two registries in the council: one for practitioners and one for specialists.

In the late 1980s, the government decided to carry out health care reforms and split the Medical and Health Department into two institutions: the Hospital Authority and the Department of Health. The Hospital Authority was established by statute, independent of the civil service and funded separately by the government, to integrate the management structures of all public and subvented hospitals in Hong Kong. In 1988, Professor Young was invited to be a member of the Provisional Hospital Authority to lay the groundwork, administrative and legal, for the Hospital Authority. When the Hospital Authority was formed in 1990, she became a member of the Hospital Authority Board. In 1989, she was appointed chairman of the Working Party on Primary Health Care to assess the status of primary care services in Hong Kong and to recommend reforms to improve them. Thus, Professor Young contributed to a spectrum of reforms that resulted in better hospital, outpatient, and preventive health services in Hong Kong.

After she stepped down as pro-vice-chancellor, Professor Young was recruited to chair the Education Commission, which was established in 1984 as recommended by the OECD (Organisation for Economic Co-operation and Development) International Panel invited by the government to look into means of improving the quality of education in Hong Kong. She was responsible for the publication of Education Commission Reports No. 6 and 7 with proposals to improve the languages of instruction, the quality of teachers, as well as quality assurance of education in Hong Kong.

Few individuals in Hong Kong have contributed so much to medical education and administration in HKU, and medical services and general education in the community at large for so long. It is not surprising that she has received numerous awards and honours from her alma mater and other universities in Hong Kong, and from the governments of both the former and the present administration for her dedicated and distinguished public service.

This book is prepared to commemorate Professor Young's seventieth year of service to HKU in 2023 and to honour her for her loyalty and devotion to serve the university and the community. It is organized into two parts with six chapters. Part 1 has three chapters, Professor Young's life story in three stages chronologically: from birth to fifteen years; her secondary, university, and postgraduate education; and her career in medicine, administration, and public service. Part 2 is a thematic approach to her contributions in administration to HKU and in the field of medicine and educational policy to the community in three separate chapters. Her life stories and accomplishments are described in the context of the socioeconomic backdrop in Hong Kong at the time.

The word 'service' usually means a system that provides something that the public needs, organized by the government or a private agency. The definition does not indicate whether the public has to pay for the service or not, or whether the service has been given free of charge by the provider and not the institution he or she represents. I felt the need to explain the nature of the service provided by Professor Young, as indicated in the title of the book: *Rosie Young: A Lifetime of Selfless Service*. After graduation, Professor Young was employed by HKU to provide clinical service, teaching, and research in the Department of Medicine. Her initial public service in medicine began when she was a member of the Medical Council in 1978, and the work did not occupy much of her time then. By the late 1980s, her public service work had grown to be so enormous that she had to give up her clinical and research work. Because she felt she was unable to perform her duties fully, she voluntarily requested the university to reduce her salary by half. As a result, her public service work was not paid for by anyone or any institution. After retirement, she continued her public service work in the same manner. In fact, all her services to the community from the late 1980s had been given voluntarily and freely with dedication. We are all grateful for her wisdom, generosity, and altruism to provide a better life for the citizens of Hong Kong.

The background information for this book was drawn from primary sources: Colonial Office archives, Hong Kong Government reports, annual and special reports produced by the Hong Kong Medical and Health Department, HKU reports and websites, Hong Kong government websites, and newspapers such as *South China Morning Post*. Secondary sources include a number of books and journals. The personal information on Professor Young and her work at HKU have been obtained from interviews that I conducted with Professor Young in person and online, as well as my personal contact with her first as a student and then as a colleague in recent years. Since the minutes of the University Council, Senate, and the Faculty of Medicine are not in the public domain, I have relied on information from the reports of HKU and what Professor Young was able to provide. I do not claim to know Professor Young well, but I believe few people do. Most of us admire her from a distance. The manuscript has been reviewed by Professor Young for accuracy. Finally, I wish to stress that the opinions expressed in this book are entirely my own.

Moira Chan-Yeung
Vancouver
October 2023

Acknowledgements

I wish to thank Professor Fung Yee Wang and Professor Wong Tai Wai for reviewing the manuscript and for their valuable suggestions. My sincere gratitude goes to Dr Chan Wai Man for obtaining information about primary health care in Hong Kong and for her most helpful suggestions and meticulous proofreading. I am much obliged to Professor Bernadette Tsui, Mr Henry Wai, and Mrs Veronica Ho of HKU for their invaluable advice and for providing various information and statistics of the university from 1948 to 1999 and the committees participated in by Professor Young when she was sub-dean, dean of the Faculty of Medicine, and pro-vice-chancellor of HKU. Lastly, I wish to thank Mr Stanley Yeung for his assistance in organizing the Zoom meetings and for obtaining photographs from various sources; Ms Carlina Ng for her help in forwarding materials; and the Department of Medicine, the Faculty of Medicine, and HKU Archives for permission to reproduce some photographs. I am, of course, most indebted to Professor Rosie Young for her patience in spending so many hours of interviews, in answering my numerous emails, and providing photographs.

Author's Note

After some deliberation I have decided to address Professor Rosie Young in the first part of the book as Rosie and as Professor Young from the time she was promoted to professor of medicine at HKU. Doctors were addressed as professors after their promotion to professorship. In this book, all photographs without a specified source were provided by Professor Young.

Part 1

1
Childhood

A Journey to the 'Pearl of the Orient': Rosie's Parents

It was a beautiful sunny day in June 1912. A gentle breeze lessened the early summer heat. The pier in Shiqi (Zhongshan) was packed with a noisy crowd. Travellers waiting to board the huge junk for Hong Kong were saying their farewells to tearful wives and children. When the time finally came for boarding, the men picked up their belongings and pressed forward to the gangway, half-pushed and half-carried. As the junk began its glide down the river, the travellers settled on the deck, chatting loudly to each other. Most of them were labourers, bound for faraway places in Southeast Asia, North America, or Australia, leaving to seek their fortune like many before them—all part of the Chinese diaspora. Since China's Qing government regarded emigration as illegal, emigrants used Hong Kong, a place ceded to Britain at the mouth of the Pearl River Delta, as a stepping-stone in their journey to their final destinations. By the beginning of the twentieth century, transportation between the various counties in southern Guangdong and Hong Kong had become more frequent, initially by junk and later by steamship. Vessels departed daily, leaving in the morning from ports such as Shiqi, and arriving in Hong Kong that afternoon.

Over the centuries, emigration from China's coastal provinces to other parts of the world was not uncommon. It escalated during the latter half of the nineteenth century, more and more adventurous young men leaving their villages to seek their livelihood elsewhere. The prosperity that characterized the rule of the first few Manchu emperors of the Qing dynasty in the previous two centuries had created a surge in population, from 200 to 450 million in agrarian China. But the failure to improve food production in the country led to an inability to feed the mounting population. The First Opium War and the subsequent signing of many unequal treaties with foreign powers depleted the treasury of the Qing court. The resulting poverty, the corrupt and declining power of the Qing dynasty, and the unrest caused by the Taiping Rebellion spurred an unprecedented outflow of Chinese emigrants. The exodus was hastened by the discovery of gold in California in the US and in Australia.

That morning in June 1912, a young man stood alone on the deck of the huge junk. His long clean robe and his round dark-rimmed glasses betrayed his scholarly status. He was deep in thought, oblivious to the noisy chatter around him. His journey would be much shorter. He was only travelling as far as Hong Kong, where he hoped to realize his dream.

Shiqi, the village this young man and many others on the boat came from, is situated about ninety kilometres south of Guangzhou and about forty kilometres north of Macao in the great delta of the Pearl River, which originates in Yunnan province and coils through Guangxi and Guangdong provinces. This long West River is joined by two tributaries, North River and East River, before emptying into the sea. In those days marshes and rice fields stretched between Shiqi and Macao. In 1879, a fourteen-year-old boy who would become a famous leader left his village, Cuiheng, in Zhongshan, for distant Hawaii to live with his brother.[1] His name was Sun Yat-sen. Sun went to school in Hawaii and returned to China a few years later. He entered the Hong Kong College of Medicine in 1887, when the college first opened, and graduated in 1892, ranking first in a class of two with high marks in all subjects. It was during his student days in

---

1. Marie-Claire Bergère, *Sun Yat-Sen*, trans. Janet Lloyd (Stanford, CA: Stanford University Press, 1994), 23–24.

Hong Kong that Sun first conceived the idea of a revolution to overthrow the corrupt Qing government. After graduation, instead of continuing his medical practice in Macao, Sun decided he wanted to heal his sick country instead of his sick country folks. The first attempt to take over Guangzhou in 1895 failed, as did several subsequent attempts. However, the ignominious defeat of China by Japan in the First Sino-Japanese War in 1894–1895;[2] the failed Hundred Days' Reform of Emperor Guangxu in 1899;[3] the ill-fated Boxer Rebellion in 1900, which resulted in the Eight Nation Alliance Army entering Beijing; and the hasty evacuation of the Qing imperial court from Beijing to Xian,[4] persuaded many to support the revolution and sounded the death knell for the Qing dynasty.

Yeung Shun Hang (楊巽行), the scholarly young man on his way to Hong Kong in June 1912, was the youngest of six in his family, with three elder brothers and two sisters. His father, a scholar or *xiucai* (秀才)[5] turned businessman, descended from a long line of scholars. The family prospered until Shun Hang's father was forced into bankruptcy when a friend for whom he was the guarantor defaulted on a huge loan. This ended Shun Hang's original ambition of future studies abroad. When the Republic of China was founded with Dr Sun Yat-sen as its first president on 1 January 1912, Shun Hang was overjoyed. Like many other patriotic young men, he wanted to serve the people and help Sun to build a strong China. He decided that after his graduation from the district middle school, he would continue his studies in Hong Kong, where Sun had received his education.

After the Boxer Rebellion fiasco, Empress Dowager Cixi saw the wisdom of reforming the government, including the educational system.

---

2. History of War, First Sino-Japanese War (1894–1895), accessed 22 February 2023, http://www.historyofwar.org/articles/wars_first_sino_japanese.html.
3. Meribeth E. Cameron, *The Reform Movement in China 1899–1912* (Stanford, CA: Stanford University Press, 1931), 23–35.
4. Cameron, *The Reform Movement*, 40.
5. A scholar who passed the entry-level exam, which enabled him to sit for a higher level of examinations in ancient China. The concept of choosing bureaucrats by merits and not by birth began in the Tang dynasty (618–907) and abolished by the late Qing dynasty in 1905. In some dynasties in between, *xiucai*s were called by a different name.

In 1901, she and her court put in place a system of schools for Western learning similar to those ordered by the deposed Emperor Guangxu in his Hundred Days' Reform in 1899. The school system in China from 1904 to 1912 was structured as follows:

> Kindergarten: one year
> Lower primary school: five years
> Higher primary school: four years
> Middle school: five years
> Higher school: three years
> University: four years[6]

Shun Hang would have carried on with the next stage of education in his home province of Guangdong had not the Xinhai revolution broken out in October 1911, followed by uprisings in the provinces. After the founding of the Republic of China, even though a government was set up in Guangzhou under the Kuomintang (KMT), unrest persisted in many parts of the province.[7]

Before Shun Hang left for Hong Kong, his mother had insisted that he should get married. The average life expectancy was only forty years, so most young men were expected to marry and start a family by the age of seventeen. Shun Hang had no say in the choice of his bride but had to trust the judgement of his mother. Usually, the groom would not meet the bride until the day of the wedding. Shun Hang and his bride had met, however, because they attended the same *sishu* (私塾) or a small private school, as children.

Siu Shui Ying (蕭瑞英), a pretty girl from the same village, was a year younger than Shun Hang. Her father, a wealthy man, had made his fortune in Hong Kong. Although Shun Hang's father had lost his business and his money, his scholarly lineage made up for the lack of means as the match was considered.

Shui Ying's feet were bound since she was young, which reflected the economic status of the family. Foot-binding (bound feet were also known

---

6. 顧樹森：《中國歷代教育制度》（南京：江蘇人民出版社，1981），242。
7. Michael Tsin, *Nation, Governance, and Modernity in China* (Stanford, CA: Sanford University Press, 1999), 55–56.

as 'lotus feet'), was a cruel ancient custom of applying tight binding to the feet of young girls to prevent further growth. All the toes except the big toe were bent under the sole and the feet were kept bound at all times to prevent them from recovering. This custom caused excruciating pain and chronic infection, even gangrene. Under China's Confucian culture, a woman had no legal rights and was subjugated to her father at birth, her husband after marriage, and her son during widowhood. Since 'it is the virtue of a woman to be without talent' in Confucianism, women were denied education. In those days, girls were not accepted by the village *sishu*. The *sishu* in Shiqi was opened by Shun Hang's uncle, another *xiucai*. Shui Ying's father, however, a progressive man for his time, insisted that Shui Ying go to the village *sishu*. Therefore, Shui Ying was carried on her maid's back every day to school until she had completed her primary education.

Alone for the first time after days of bidding farewell to his relatives, his friends, his parents and in-laws, and his new wife, Shun Hang had a chance to reflect on his future. Marriage was not something that he would have liked at this stage of his life because of his own uncertain future. Nevertheless, over the two months since his marriage, he had begun to develop feelings for Shui Ying. Moreover, he would no longer be totally on his own in a strange new place. Having a father-in-law who possessed blocks of houses in Hong Kong meant that it was likely he would have a roof over his head until he was able to fend for himself.

The reformed school system was new for China and school budgets were meagre. Schools were short of teachers, especially those who could teach English, and there were few textbooks. At the recommendation of his younger brother-in-law, Shun Hang entered Queen's College in Hong Kong, previously Central School, to brush up on his English and other subjects. The Central School, the oldest government secondary school in Hong Kong, had been established in 1862 by the British colonial government as an Anglo-Chinese secondary school. It was initially located at Gough Street, Sheung Wan. In 1884, it expanded to a new site at Aberdeen Street and Hollywood Road and was renamed Victoria College. Ten years later, the name was changed again, to Queen's College. The school taught both Chinese and Western subjects, including arithmetic, geography, hygiene, history, and general intelligence, and had a programme of extra-curricular activities, lacking in many schools in Hong Kong at the time. Because the government used it as a model for other schools, Queen's College had a larger operating budget and offered higher salaries for teachers.[8]

Shun Hang successfully entered the Faulty of Arts at the University of Hong Kong (HKU) after one year at Queen's College. He had wanted to study political science, but HKU did not have such a faculty or department. At the time, students at HKU were usually required to live in a residence hall, but Shun Hang obtained an exemption because he had no means of paying the high residence fees. His father-in-law had always been generous and kind and invited Shun Hang to live in the family's spacious home.

The newly established university was considered a place for the wealthy. Shun Hang's academic standing was not high enough to earn him a scholarship, and he did not wish to ask his father-in-law to support him. Instead, he studied hard and worked even harder tutoring younger students. Shun Hang was an excellent student himself, but he did not have adequate time for his studies. Every day after lectures, he rushed off to tutor, and he spent most weekends doing the same to come up with the university fees. During his final year, he failed one subject and so was unable to graduate.

Greatly disappointed, Shun Hang re-evaluated his life. By then, he was twenty-two with a wife and a child living in his parents' home in Shiqi. After five years in Hong Kong, he had not yet established himself. Should he spend another year at university to obtain his degree? Should he forget about university and take up his responsibilities as a husband and a father? Without a certificate of graduation,[9] the chances of getting a good job in Hong Kong were less favourable, but he could certainly make a living by

---

8. Hong Kong Blue Book, Education, 1888 and 1889.
9. There were two documents to show Yeung Shun Hang's attendance in HKU as a student. The first one is the critique of his composition by Professor Lai Chai Hei (Figure 1.2). The second one is the presence of his name as one of the editors of HKU magazine, in Peter Cunich's book, *A History of the University of Hong Kong: Volume 1, 1911–1945* (Hong Kong: Hong Kong University Press, 2012), 490.

Figure 1.1: The University of Hong Kong in 1912. Source: HKU Archives.

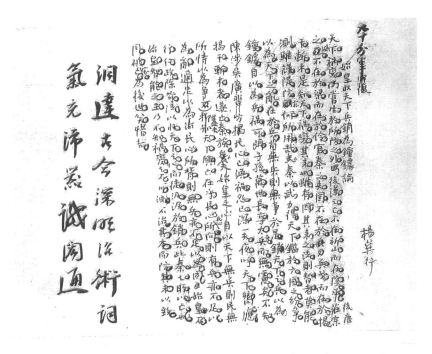

Figure 1.2: Critique of Yeung Shun Hang's composition by Professor Lai Chai Hei of HKU—a record of Shun Hang's attendance at HKU.

becoming a teacher or by tutoring, and he was not confident he would be able to pass his examination even after another year of study. What if he failed again? After many hours of vacillation, he decided to leave the university and seek work in Hong Kong. His decision was also influenced by the fact that his dream of returning to China to help the new republic had been dashed.

In 1912, Sun Yat-sen had yielded the presidency to Yuan Shikai, a military official of the Qing court who had risen to power and forced the abdication of the last monarch of the Qing dynasty. Yuan's rule became increasingly autocratic as he gained executive authority. His short presidency was complicated; briefly, he weakened the national assembly and attempted to eradicate the KMT. In 1915, Yuan endeavoured to return China to a monarchy, proposing himself as the Hongxian emperor. Vigorous opposition from all over the country forced him to give up this plan, and he died the following year. Yuan's death led to the fragmentation of the country, and China degenerated into the warlord period.[10] The general expectation among the Chinese elite that the situation would improve after the revolution had evaporated.

Figure 1.3a: Rosie's father, Yeung Shun Hang.

Figure 1.3b: Rosie's mother, Siu Shui Ying.

---

10. Ernest Young, *The Presidency of Yuan Shikai: Liberalism and Dictatorship in Early Republican China* (Ann Arbor: The University of Michigan Press, 1977), 222–40.

Once Shun Hang had made up his mind to settle in Hong Kong, his brother-in-law offered him a position in his company, recognizing his abilities. Shun Hang returned to Shiqi to collect his wife and child. In the summer of 1917, the family began a new life in Hong Kong.

The House on On Lan (安蘭) Street

Sau Han (秀嫻, Rosie) was born on 23 October 1930, the fifth and the last child of Shun Hang's family. Shui Ying, although having grown up in a family steeped in ancient Chinese customs, embraced the modern idea of having fewer children and spacing them. The family's first son, Wai Lam (偉林), was born in 1915; the second son, Woon Lam (煥林), in 1917; the third son, Ho Lam (浩林), in 1920; and the first daughter, Sau Man (秀文, Pauline), in 1924. Rosie was delivered by Wong Ye-gu, the most celebrated midwife in Hong Kong.[11] Decades later, Rosie would work alongside one of Wong Ye-gu's grandchildren, Dr Joseph Pan, a well-known cardiologist.

In the early 1930s, Hong Kong was recovering from the financial disaster caused by the strike-boycott of 1925–1926[12] and the Great Depression which had affected the world in 1929–1930. By then the city had also shed its infamous insanitary image to become one of the cleanest cities in East Asia. The horrendous plague of 1894 had served as a wake-up call for the government and the people of Hong Kong to pay greater attention to sanitation. The government made special efforts to reduce infant and maternal mortality by training midwives in the Western

---

11. Moira Chan-Yeung, *A Medical History of Hong Kong: The Development and Contributions of Outpatient Services* (Hong Kong: Chinese University of Hong Kong Press, 2021), 134–40.
12. The May 31 incident in 1925 occurred when a Japanese foreman killed a Chinese worker in a cotton factory in the Shanghai International Settlement. Students and workers protested outside a British Police Station against this killing, when British police opened fire and killed a number of protestors. Workers and students in Shanghai went on strike and called for a national strike. The strike-boycott in 1925–1926 was called when the British soldiers opened fire at protesting workers and students in Shamian in June 1925. Hong Kong workers responded to the call of a strike-boycott which started in June 1925 and lasted for about sixteen months, causing disastrous effects on Hong Kong's economy.

method of delivery and placing them in charge of domiciliary services. In 1921, the government also began a school health programme first for students of government schools and later for all grant schools.[13] Students received health examinations and free dental care and eyeglasses if they needed them. School premises were also inspected for ventilation, lighting, sanitation, water supply, space, desks and seats, state of repair, and the number of students allowed.[14]

Rosie's family lived in a rented house on On Lan Street, in the Central District of Hong Kong. Shui Ying's parents had given her a house in Kowloon Tong as part of her dowry, but since Kowloon was an inconvenient place to live with five school-aged children and inadequate transportation, the Kowloon house was rented out for income. On Lan Street is a short and narrow street that runs parallel to Queen's Road Central, connecting Wyndham Street on the west and Zetland Street on the east. Although it is a street with office buildings now, it was a residential area in the busy Central District during Rosie's happy childhood.

In those days, only the wealthy European houses in Hong Kong had water closets. The homes of wealthy Chinese families and some Europeans had dry latrines, which were only for men. Women and children of all classes used pots, generally kept under their beds. The pots were emptied into a large bucket, the contents of which (referred to as night soil) were collected in the early hours of the morning by unskilled female labourers and carried to the waterfront, where the contents were emptied into boats at specified points before six o'clock in the morning. The government contractor provided junks to transport the night soil from private houses and public latrines, government buildings, and jails to Guangzhou or somewhere else in China, where it was sold as fertilizer. Occupants of private houses paid a small sum for the night soil removal services. Before the Second World War, the charge for daily removal (usually available only to Europeans and wealthy Chinese), was $0.5 to $1 per month; for removal

---

13. *Medical and Sanitary Report for the Year 1921*, Hong Kong Administrative Report 1921, M(1)22.
14. *Medical and Sanitary Report for the Year 1929*, Hong Kong Administrative Report 1929, M37.

every second day, the monthly cost per family was $0.3 to $0.4. The government contractor also supplied a street-sweeping crew. The rubbish was taken by boat to Lap Sap Wan (Gin Drinkers Bay), where it was simply thrown on the beach.[15]

Bathing was done in the bathroom or in the kitchen. Piped-in hot water was unheard of. In cold weather, water from a heated kettle was poured into a big wooden basin and mixed with cold water until the temperature was suitable for bathing. From this basin of water, a small wooden bucket was used to pour water onto the body. Perishable food was purchased once or twice a day, because no one had a refrigerator. Wood had to be bought and carried to the house to provide fuel for cooking. Then there was the problem of laundry, house cleaning, and the numerous other tasks that required manual labour.

In those days, everyday living required a great deal of work. How did Shui Ying manage such a large family with her bound feet? Coming from a well-to-do family, she had brought with her to Hong Kong several *mui tsai*s, who had served her before her marriage. *Mui tsai* (妹仔), which means 'little sister' in Cantonese, was the term for young Chinese women who worked as domestic servants.[16] Typically from poor families, they were sold at a young age to wealthy families on the condition that they be freed through marriage when they were old enough. Such arrangements were generally looked upon as charitable because these girls were better provided for as *mui tsai* than they would have been otherwise.[17] In consideration of China's grinding poverty, this was seen as an acceptable arrangement for unwanted girls though the absence of contracts in some cases also meant that *mui tsai*s might be resold into prostitution.

---

15. *Oswald Chadwick's Report on the Sanitary Condition of Hong Kong with Appendices and Plans*. Eastern No. 38, Printed for the use of the Colonial Office November, 1882, CO 882, 18–21; P. S. Selwyn-Clarke, *Report on Medical and Health Conditions in Hong Kong for the Period 1 January 1941 to 31 August 1945* (London: His Majesty's Stationery Office, 1946), 8–10.
16. Anti–Mui Tsai Society meetings, *South China Morning Post*, 11 April 1927, 14 October 1927, 18 December 1932, and 1 August 1933.
17. Smith, Carl T., *A Sense of History: Studies of the Social and Urban History of Hong Kong* (Hong Kong: Hong Kong Educational Publishing Co., 1995), 243–51.

The establishment of the Republic of China in 1912 brought changing social values, and women's issues rose in the public's consciousness. While the thousands of missionaries who poured into China after the First Opium War in the Treaty Ports made few inroads with their agenda of Christian conversion, they greatly influenced Chinese cultural attitudes toward women. The missionaries saw education and abolition of foot-binding as the keys to women's emancipation. They formed anti-foot-binding societies to help eradicate the practice that kept women completely at the disposal of men. In addition, missionaries supported the anti–*mui tsai* movement in Hong Kong and Shanghai. In 1921, Chinese Christians in Hong Kong formed the Anti–Mui Tsai Society. Although the Anti–Mui Tsai Bill was passed in 1923,[18] it was not until the 1930s that *mui tsai*s were finally free to leave their mistresses. Those who wished to stay on in a household had to be paid a regular wage.[19] In the Yeung household, at least two *mui tsai*s remained as domestic helpers during the Second World War.

Rosie was assigned the name Sau Han by her father at birth, but the name did not appeal to her. In light of this, before she entered primary school, her father gave her another name, Tse Tse (紫芝), after a well-known Chinese poet in the Song dynasty.[20] Although the poet was a man, the Chinese characters in the name were more frequently used in women's names. At the age of six, like other children, Rosie began her schooling, attending Tai Yuk Primary School, a private school near her house. The school had been established in 1908 by Dr Ho Ko Tsun, a graduate of the Hong Kong College of Medicine, and his friends. The premises served as a primary school during the day and offered classes for sports training in the

---

18. Smith, *A Sense of History*, 254–65.
19. 'Anti–*Mui-Tsai* Bill', *South China Morning Post*, 1 August 1933.
20. 周紫芝（1082–1155年），字少隱，號竹坡居士，宣城（今安徽宣城市）人，南宋文學家。以詩著名，也能詞，譬如《踏莎行》寫離人別情：「遊絲飛絮，斜陽煙渚，愁情無數。」給人的感覺是情深意切，景物迷離。堪稱難得的上乘之作。其中「淚珠閣定空相覻」一句的用詞尤其巧妙，最後這一問更是催人淚下。其他如《生查子》、《西江月》、《菩薩蠻》、《謁金門》、《蔔運算元》等都是佳作。著有《太倉梯米集》七十卷、《竹坡詩話》一卷、《竹坡詞》三卷。存詞150首。

evening. Dr Ho was honorary principal of the primary school and elected president of the sports training organization. He also taught hygiene and first aid in the school.[21] Ho secretly supported Dr Sun Yat-sen's revolutionary endeavours,[22] and Rosie's father, a patriot, must have sent her to this school so she could learn more about their homeland. At the turn of the twentieth century, Hong Kong was a haven for revolutionaries. The headquarters for the *South China Morning Post*, an English newspaper first published on 6 November 1903, was only a block from the Yeungs' residence. One of the paper's two founders, Tse Tsan-tai (謝纘泰), was determined to bring down the teetering Qing dynasty.

Rosie graduated from Primary 6 from Tai Yuk Primary School at the age of ten. Because she was hoping to go to university, she followed in her sister's footsteps and entered Class 7 of the Anglo-Chinese Sacred Heart School (renamed Sacred Heart Canossian College in 1960) in September 1940. The Canossian sisters called Rosie's sister Pauline, and they had romanized her last name to Young. The Canossian sisters changed Rosie's name as well to Rosie Young. All certificates and diplomas from then on showed her name as Young Tse Tse, Rosie. The change of name would cause recurrent troubles to Rosie later in life. For example, on her Hong Kong identification card, her name appeared as Yeung Tse Tse. During a sabbatical leave in San Francisco on a fellowship from the China Medical Board, she was unable to cash a cheque because it was made payable to Young Tse Tse, Rosie, but her name in the passport was Yeung Tse Tse, Rosie.

A Natural Talent

As the youngest in the family, Rosie received considerable attention from her parents. Lively, clever, and endowed with an excellent memory, she could recite the multiplication tables long before she entered primary school. But still, Wai Lam, a boy and the eldest, was the apple of her father's eye.

---

21. 清何高俊撰，《赤十字會初級急救要法》，香港聚珍書樓鉛印本，清光緒三十四年。
22. 〈何高俊醫生逝世〉, *Wah Kiu Yat Po*, 7 June 1953.

Wai Lam entered HKU when Rosie was only three years old. Following in the footsteps of his father, he took secondary schooling at Queen's College, earning the highest marks in the school on his matriculation examination. He was offered a full government scholarship if he would enter the Faculty of Arts and aim for government service on graduation—an attractive proposal. But Wai Lam had long desired to become a doctor. That meant his father would have to support him for six more years, but Shun Hang had no qualms about working harder on behalf of his beloved son. He took on more students for tutoring. As expected, Wai Lam excelled academically in almost all his subjects, graduating from the Faculty of Medicine in 1939. During his student days, Wai Lam and his future wife, the daughter of an affluent family, took Rosie to the luxurious Peninsula Hotel[23] for high tea one afternoon, giving her a taste of the pleasure wealth could bring.

Wai Lam began working as a doctor in Tung Wah Hospital, which had been established in 1872 with a government grant and donations from the local Chinese elite. It was a hospital for Chinese, using only Chinese treatments by traditional Chinese medicine practitioners during the early days of its establishment.[24] Western medicine was gradually introduced to the hospital after 1896. Doctors from the Hong Kong College of Medicine and later from HKU worked in Tung Wah Hospital as resident doctors. Shortly after, Wai Lam established his own private practice.

Rosie adored her second brother, Woon Lam, who often looked after her. Because of her bound feet, their mother, Shui Ying, was unable to carry out the duties of a modern-day parent. Woon Lam took Rosie out to play and ensured that she completed her homework. He also took her shopping for clothing and other daily needs. When one of the family's *mui tsai*s injured her leg and was unable to walk, Woon Lam carried her on his back to see a Chinese medicine doctor every day until she recovered. A gentle, kind, and compassionate boy, Woon Lam was his mother's

---

23. The Peninsula Hong Kong is a colonial-style hotel located in Tsim Sha Tsui, Kowloon. The hotel, which opened in 1928, is still regarded as one of the most luxurious hotels in Hong Kong.
24. MacDonnell to Earl of Kimberley, Chinese Hospital, 19 February 1872, CO 129/156 #947, 339.

favourite. He was also a talented student who entered medical school before the Second World War.

Rosie was a loner and had few childhood friends. Other than reading, her favourite pastime was to play school. She would recruit the *mui tsai*s who were not busy as her students. She taught them reading and writing using a blackboard and a few pieces of chalk. When people asked what she wanted to be when she grew up, Rosie had no hesitation in saying that she wanted to be a politician like Dr Sun Yat-sen, so that she could save the country, or a scientist, so that she could save humankind and win a Nobel Prize.

It is not difficult to understand why Rosie, daughter of a patriot, who wished to become a politician to serve in Dr Sun Yat-sen's administration to save his homeland, and educated in a patriotic primary school, would have the same dream as her father. It is less clear why she wanted to be a scientist and a Nobel Prize winner. The subsequent turbulent years of the Sino-Japanese War, the Second World War, the civil war between the KMT and the Chinese Communist Party (CCP) leading to the founding of the People's Republic of China in 1949, followed by years of unrest in the country, thwarted her chances to be educated in the disciplines that would lead to the fulfilment of her dreams to be a politician or a scientist. Instead, she developed and fully utilized her talents in other areas but with the ultimate aim of serving humanity.

Shui Ying's sisters had married well-to-do men, so Rosie and her siblings had wealthy cousins. The Yeung family was proud, however, and was never ashamed of their relative 'poverty'. Rosie did not mind wearing the hand-me-down clothes from her cousins. On weekends, Woon Lam tutored their cousins at home, and Rosie always sat in on the lessons. She invariably completed her assignments well and presented the results neatly. On one occasion, when Woon Lam complimented one of the cousins on her work but failed to praise Rosie, Rosie began to cry. Afterwards, Woo Lam explained to his sister that her work had been perfect, and he expected nothing short of that. However, since her cousin had shown considerable improvement, it was vital to encourage her so she would continue to do better. Rosie never forgot his wise words, and she would apply them to her own teaching in the future

CANOSSIAN CONVENT
SACRED HEART SCHOOL
HONG KONG.

SCHOOL REPORT and CERTIFICATE
of the Scholastic Year 1940-41.

Name Rosie Young, Tsi Tsee
Class 7A
Admitted to the School in 1940

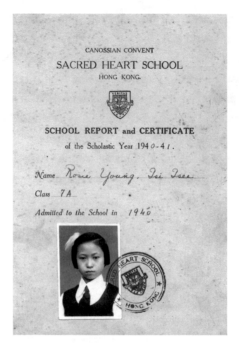

Figure 1.4a: Rosie's Sacred Heart School Report (front page) 1940–1941.

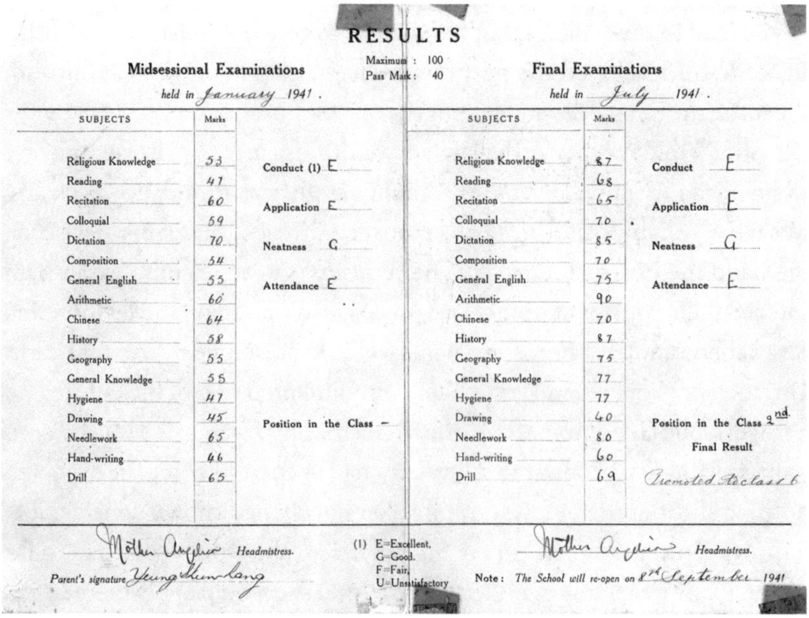

RESULTS

Maximum : 100
Pass Mark : 40

Midsessional Examinations held in January 1941.

SUBJECTS	Marks	
Religious Knowledge	53	Conduct (1) E
Reading	47	
Recitation	60	Application E
Colloquial	59	
Dictation	70	Neatness G
Composition	54	
General English	55	Attendance E
Arithmetic	60	
Chinese	64	
History	58	
Geography	55	
General Knowledge	55	
Hygiene	47	
Drawing	45	Position in the Class –
Needlework	65	
Hand-writing	46	
Drill	65	

Mother Angelica Headmistress.
Parent's signature Yeung Shun-lang

(1) E=Excellent, G=Good. F=Fair, U=Unsatisfactory

Final Examinations held in July 1941.

SUBJECTS	Marks	
Religious Knowledge	87	Conduct E
Reading	68	
Recitation	65	Application E
Colloquial	70	
Dictation	85	Neatness G
Composition	70	
General English	75	Attendance E
Arithmetic	90	
Chinese	70	
History	87	
Geography	75	
General Knowledge	77	
Hygiene	77	
Drawing	40	Position in the Class 2nd
Needlework	80	Final Result
Hand-writing	60	
Drill	69	Promoted to class 6

Mother Angelica Headmistress.
Note: The School will re-open on 8th September 1941

Figure 1.4b: Rosie's Sacred Heart School Report (second and third pages) in 1940–1941.

In the early 1930s, while China was caught up in civil war, Japan, seeking raw materials to fuel its expanding industries, took over Manchuria.[25] Japan then gradually infiltrated north China, occupying more and more areas in the north. The KMT, the ruling party, and the CCP were also fighting, and the KMT opted at first to eliminate the CCP rather than fight against the Japanese. After an incident on 7 July 1937, when there was an exchange of fire between China's National Revolutionary Army and the Imperial Japanese Army at the Marco Polo Bridge near Beijing, China finally declared war on Japan. The Marco Polo incident is generally regarded as the beginning of the Second Sino-Japanese War. The Japanese army marched south, taking over the coastal area of China. In October 1938, it seized Guangzhou. The war sent refugees streaming southwards, Hong Kong receiving about 740,000 of them during those two years.

This influx affected many households in Hong Kong. During 1938, the Yeung residence was overcrowded with relatives, adults and children, from the mainland. Rosie's father welcomed his relatives to stay until they were able to find jobs and a place to live. One day, one of the older boys teased Rosie until she was in tears. When this brought more taunting, Rosie flew into a rage and chased the boy onto the street, creating a scene. The noise drew her father downstairs. He took Rosie aside and when she had calmed down, he told her gently that her behaviour was not acceptable. When others fell into unfortunate circumstances, he counselled, you should treat them with respect, not make them feel worse. Moreover, it was not proper for a girl to run into the street, threatening to beat up a boy! What she should have done was to ignore him. This valuable conversation remained with Rosie for the rest of her life.

Japanese Invasion and Occupation

On 8 December 1941, Japan invaded Hong Kong, simultaneously bombing Pearl Harbor, without officially declaring war against either the British Empire or the United States. The Second World War ended Rosie's

---

25. Manchuria refers to a region in northeastern China that consisted of three provinces—Heilongjiang, Jilin, and Liaoning. The term is no longer used.

happy childhood, ushering her into maturity in the course of the next few months.

The battle-hardened Japanese troops, 50,000 of them, marched across the border into the New Territories, easily breaking through the Gin Drinker's line that was supposed to contain them for at least three days. The Hong Kong garrison, consisting of British, Indian, and Canadian units, the Auxiliary Defence Units, and the Hong Kong Volunteer Defence Corps, totalled around 14,500, mostly young men without military training. They fought bravely for seventeen days before Sir Mark Young, the Hong Kong governor and commander-in-chief, surrendered on Christmas Day, marking the beginning of a period of brutal Japanese rule of three years and eight months.[26]

When the Japanese bombing began, the Yeung family left their home at the urging of Wai Lam, to take shelter at Tung Wah Hospital. Wai Lam was a resident doctor there and had a room. He believed that hospitals should be spared from bombing. Instead of going to the air raid shelter, the family left the house in a hurry on any rickshaw that they could find. Rosie shared one with her father, sitting on his lap. That evening, Rosie heard the shrieking sound of a siren. All the lights were off and the curtains drawn. Around the edges of the curtains, Rosie could see two powerful searchlights flickering in the sky. There were several short bursts of gunfire, then a bang so loud that her eardrums almost burst. They learned later that the wall next to their room had been hit by a stray bullet. Had it struck any closer, some of her family would have been hurt or killed. By then, the Japanese army had reached Kowloon and was shelling from across the harbour.[27] After the Hong Kong government surrendered, the Yeung family returned to On Lan Street and remained there for the duration of the war.

The people of Hong Kong now lived under a highly repressive regime. Their conquerors inflicted appalling suffering. People feared the

---

26. S. Tsang, *A Modern History of Hong Kong* (Hong Kong: Hong Kong University Press, 2004), 119–24.
27. Kate Whitehead, 'Rosie Young, HKU Medic 1953', in *Confessions and Professions: Grand Rounds in Hong Kong Medicine*, ed. Madeline Slavick and Anna Koor (Hong Kong: MCCM Creations), 23.

Kempeitai, the military police force, which used prisoners as targets for shooting, beheading, and bayonet practice.[28] Ordinary citizens were subjected to humiliation every time they passed a Japanese military post, where bowing to the guards was mandatory.

The Japanese did not wish to be responsible for the livelihood of refugees from China, whose presence had increased the city's population from about 1 million to 1.7 million. The occupying force did the simplest thing they could to ease the strain—sent anyone who was not a Hong Kong resident back to mainland China.[29] To monitor the repatriation process, a census was carried out in February 1942[30] and annually thereafter. The census gave the Japanese a clear idea of the size of the population, identified 'undesirable' characters,[31] and determined who would receive ration cards for everyday necessities such as rice, sugar, and peanut oil.

The census was carried out by the Japanese most expeditiously. On the given morning, all the occupants of a house, both adults and children, were ordered to stand in rows in front of the house while the Japanese official counted their numbers. Houses were also searched to make sure no one was hiding. The procedure took fifteen to twenty minutes for each house.[32] The census caused families with young women great anxiety. The women of the household would smear dirt on their faces, dress in shabby clothes, and cast their eyes downwards to avoid the notice of Japanese officials. There were rumours of rape and of young women being kidnapped to become comfort women.[33]

Due to repatriation, the population of Hong Kong dropped sharply, falling back to one million by September 1942.[34] The decline continued

---

28. Jenny Chan and Derek Pua, *Three Years Eight Months: The Forgotten Struggle of Hong Kong's WWII* (San Francisco, CA: Pacific Atrocities Education, 2017), 74–75; J. M. Carroll, *A Concise History of Hong Kong* (Lanham, MD: Rowman and Littlefield, 2007), 123–29.
29. 'Repatriation of Chinese', *Hong Kong News*, 2 February 1942.
30. 'Partial Hong Kong Census Returns', *Hong Kong News*, 10 February 1942.
31. 'Census of Population', *Hong Kong News*, 30 April 1943.
32. 'Census Completed in Less Than Three Hours', *Hong Kong News*, 14 March 1944.
33. Chan and Pua, *Three Years and Eight Months*, 73.
34. 'Less than One Million Residing in Hong Kong and Kowloon', *Hong Kong News*, 29 September 1942.

over the next three years, people leaving voluntarily and others perishing from starvation or disease. By August 1945, when the Japanese surrendered, Hong Kong's population would stand at less than 600,000.

Shun Hang, as with many in Hong Kong, had no income during this time. His brother-in-law's company had closed down, and no one could afford to send their children to him for tutoring. Most of the schools were also closed, so the family was dependent on Wai Lam's salary for the duration of the war.

Rosie, at the age of eleven, found that she had become the household manager. Wai Lam was married by that time and had his own home. Woon Lam, her second brother, was in his second year of medical studies. At the onset of the Japanese occupation, the foreign staff at HKU who had joined the Hong Kong Volunteer Defence Corps became prisoners of war. Civilian foreign faculty members were placed in a camp at Stanley, a peninsula in southern Hong Kong. The university was shut down. Many students left for Free China to continue their education in the universities there.[35] Woon Lam joined Lingnan University, which was in Hong Kong then because of the war. When Lingnan Medical School moved north, medical students either stayed in Qujiang in northern Guangdong, or joined Jiangxi Medical School, where Woon Lam went. Woon Lam spent his third year at Jiangxi Medical School.[36] Ho Lam, Rosie's third brother, and her sister, Pauline, worked at whatever jobs they could find to offset the household expenses. Rosie's mother, though she wanted to help, was unable to leave the house because of her bound feet. Since Rosie's father, a Chinese gentleman, had no interest in household affairs, that left Rosie responsible for domestic affairs, including household financing and food. Two of her mother's *mui tsai*s had remained in the household as paid domestic helpers.

---

35. Dafydd Emrys Evans, *Constancy of Purpose: An Account of the Foundation and History of Hong Kong College of Medicine and the Faculty of Medicine of the University of Hong Kong 1887–1987* (Hong Kong: Hong Kong University Press, 1987), 164.
36. Wei Kei Kau, 'Lingnan University during the First Half of Twentieth Century', *Lingnan Newsletter*, September 2000, accessed 23 February 2023, http://luaa.hk/news/lnn_148.pdf.

At the onset of the occupation, the Japanese issued unnumbered currency notes in military yen (MY), valid only in Hong Kong. The exchange rate was fixed at two Hong Kong dollars to one MY on 5 January 1942, but that rate had doubled by October. All citizens were forced to convert Hong Kong dollars to MY.[37] Food was scarce and expensive. The Japanese had seized the rice stocks early and sold them at designated depots in different parts of Hong Kong and Kowloon.[38] After the first census, each family received a ration card from the district bureau allowing 0.4 catty (about 240 grams) of rice daily per person, at MY 0.13 per catty in late 1941. One family member was allowed to collect up to three days' rations for each family. Food shortages led to higher costs: the price of rice rose to MY 0.75 per catty by August 1943 and skyrocketed to MY 3 per catty by January 1944.[39] Sugar, peanut oil, and flour were also rationed. Meat and fish were scarce, so most people attempted to fill their stomachs with rice and vegetables, made more palatable by soya sauce. It might not be possible to obtain any vegetables, and a small amount of dried salted fish with rice at times was a real blessing. Many people lived hand to mouth, and the poorest were ravaged by starvation and malnutrition.

At the end of each month, when Wai Lam received his salary, he gave Rosie a portion. She went out immediately with her maids to obtain the family's ration for basics, such as rice and oil, and firewood. After calculating the sum necessary to cover these items for the rest of the month, she 'invested' what was left in buying ten to twelve tablets of sulphur drugs, the only antibiotics available, on Wai Lam's instructions. Since the price of drugs escalated fast, she was able to sell the antibiotics at a profit and use the proceeds to buy soya beans, vegetables, and a small amount of meat. In this way, although her family was often hungry, they did not starve or develop deficiency diseases such as beriberi, scurvy, and pellagra. Wai Lam's medical knowledge saved the family during the war.

---

37. G. B. Endacott, *Hong Kong Eclipse* (Hong Kong: Oxford University Press, 1978), 149.
38. '57 Depots will Handle Distribution', *Hong Kong News*, 7 March 1942.
39. Endacott, *Hong Kong Eclipse*, 120.

One day in 1943, the family received terrible news. Rosie's brother Woon Lam had been killed in a car accident in China. By that time, Woon Lam had completed the third-year curriculum at Jiangxi University Medical School and had been assigned to Cheeloo University for his clinical years. At the onset of war, Cheeloo University had moved its operations from Shandong province to Chengdu. Transportation was a challenge in wartime China. Woon Lam died instantly when the truck he was riding in, which was overloaded with supplies, overturned and rolled down a hill.[40] His family was devastated. Rosie and her mother were particularly badly shaken. For a while, Shui Ying spent most of her time in her room either sobbing or staring unseeingly into space. Rosie too felt the loss deeply

Figure 1.5: Diploma of graduation from Junior Secondary School, Kwong Wah School, July 1944.

---

40. Cunich, *A History of the University of Hong Kong*, 419.

though she was preoccupied with the ongoing task of getting enough provisions for the household. She also attempted to continue her studies. Sacred Heart School had closed, but she was able to attend Kwong Wah Middle School for six months. She graduated from the junior secondary school with a diploma before the school was closed. For the rest of the war, her father taught her Chinese, English, and mathematics at home.

When the Japanese surrendered on 15 August 1945, Rosie was not yet fifteen. The loss of her much-loved brother, the deprivation, and the heavy responsibility of keeping the family alive would have a permanent effect on her. By the end of the war, she had matured well beyond her age. Her experience during the war prepared her well to be in a position of responsibility and decision making. The empowerment from her parents even at a tender age gave her tremendous confidence.

2

Student Days

A New Dream Takes Shape

On 30 August 1945, the Royal Navy, led by the cruiser HMS *Swiftsure*, steamed into Victoria Harbour, flying the British flag, under the command of Rear Admiral C. H. J. Harcourt, to reclaim Hong Kong from the Japanese. On 19 September, Japanese forces surrendered to the British at Government House. Rear Admiral Harcourt set up a military government to rehabilitate the colony and worked with remarkable efficiency to restore stability in Hong Kong.

The population of Hong Kong had dwindled to around 600,000, and as families returned from mainland China, schooling for children became a problem. The government was unable to take immediate steps to revive education in the colony. Missionaries and conscientious private citizens stepped in to help to reopen schools as quickly as possible, recognizing the importance of not letting children and young people miss more schooling than they already had. By October, missionary schools such as the Diocesan Girls' School, Ying Wah Girls' School, Kowloon Wah Yan College, St. Stephen's Girls' College, and St. Paul's Co-Educational

College had reopened.¹ A number of schools re-established themselves during the ensuing months, including Sacred Heart School.²

Rosie had studied at Sacred Heart from October 1940 to December 1941, when the war broke out. The school had been set up by Canossian Sisters soon after their arrival in Hong Kong in 1860, as one of the earliest schools for girls.³ Rosie climbed the steep hill on Old Bailey Road to get to school at Mid-Levels on Caine Road every day. Most of her classmates also arrived on foot, carrying their heavy textbooks in rattan baskets. Nowadays, the students can take the escalator in Central District directly to Mid-Levels, or jump on a bus or into a taxi with their domestic helpers carrying their backpacks of books. It took Rosie only one more year to complete her high school education. Having the advantage of home education during the war, Rosie entered Class 2 (Secondary 5) of Sacred Heart School in October 1945 and passed the School Certificate Examination the following year.

Figure 2.1: Rosie, 1947.

---

1. Kit-ching Chan Lau and Peter Cunich, *The Impossible Dream: Hong Kong University from Foundation to Re-Establishment 1910 to 1950* (Hong Kong: Oxford University Press, 2002), 246.
2. 'Education Revived. Schools Being Re-opened All over Colony', *South China Morning Post*, 6 October 1945. Grant-in-aid schools received a grant from the government and were mostly missionary schools in Hong Kong.
3. Patricia P. K. Chiu, *A History of the Grant Schools Council: Mission, Vision, and Transformation* (Hong Kong: Grant Schools Council, 2013), 40.

Rosie had to find a new school for her Class I (matriculation or Secondary 6) education because Sacred Heart School offered classes up to Class 2 only, shortly after the war. Fortunately, Northcote Teacher Training College reopened in the fall of 1946, taking in students who wished to receive training to be a teacher. Since a number of schools, like Sacred Heart School, did not have Class 1, Northcote offered one year of Class 1 before starting the teachers' course the following year. In Northcote, Rosie studied Chinese, English, advanced mathematics, history, and general science. She passed her matriculation examinations with flying colours and was awarded a scholarship to enter the Faculty of Medicine, HKU, in September 1947.

The Faculty of Medicine had been offering classes since the previous fall, due to the great shortage of doctors after the war. However, it was not clear yet when or if HKU, the only university in the region, would fully reopen. It was uncertain at war's end whether Hong Kong would remain a British colony. The university campus had been badly damaged by both bombing and looting. The colonial government, its infrastructure also greatly damaged, had little cash to spare. Many people felt that Hong Kong did not need a university, since only 25 per cent of the students were local and their higher educational needs could be met in other ways.[4] It soon became obvious, however, that there was a great demand for university graduates in all fields of work, since few expatriates from England were willing to return to Hong Kong, and the few who were available demanded much higher salaries. Hong Kong Governor Alexander Grantham brought the institution's uncertain fate to an end by offering a special fund of HK$4 million for a re-establishment program and increasing the annual grant to $1.5 million.[5] The university was formally re-established on 7 April 1948 though the Great Hall (Loke Yew Hall) remained roofless for several years after that.

---

4. Peter Cunich, *A History of the University of Hong Kong: Volume 1, 1911–1945* (Hong Kong: Hong Kong University Press, 2012), 362–63.
5. Colonial Office, Note on present position regarding Hong Kong University, 20 December 1947, CO 129/610/1.

Figure 2.2a: The Roofless Great Hall (Loke Yew Hall) of HKU, 1945. Source: HKU Archives.

Figure 2.2b: Inside the Roofless Great Hall (Loke Yew Hall) of HKU, 1945. Source: HKU Archives.

During the early post-war years, most families in Hong Kong were poor, and schooling was costly. Men and women toiled tirelessly, working long hours for their living to send their boys to school. Girls as young as seven looked after younger siblings at home and helped with household chores. Even when Hong Kong's economy improved in the late 1950s, families who could afford it sent their boys to university, while girls, after their school certificate examinations, were expected to find work to support their brothers' education. Rosie's father was different. He knew education was important and would do his best to support his daughters and sons alike for university education if they wanted and were able to do so.

Rosie entered HKU at the age of sixteen in 1947, likely one of the youngest students to enter HKU that year among a cohort of young men and women who had missed three years and eight months of schooling due to the war. She made up her mind that she would fulfil the wish of her late brother, Woon Lam, to be a doctor. A set of human skeletons, purchased by Wai Lam and passed on to Woon Lam, was still lying in one of the family's closets. Before the war, one of her brothers would rub the skeleton with oil once a year and let Rosie play with it. Rosie had given up on her dream to be a politician or a scientist, because of the political situation in China and the lack of science in her schooling. She made up her mind to become a doctor instead. And so began her long association with the Faculty of Medicine at HKU.

Pre-clinical Years

During Rosie's undergraduate years, Hong Kong underwent marked changes. Immediately after the Second World War, civil war had broken out in China between the KMT and CCP, culminating in the establishment of the People's Republic of China in 1949. Again, refugees poured in from the mainland to Hong Kong to escape the carnage of war. This posed serious problems for housing, health care, education, and social services in Hong Kong. The government lacked the resources to deal with such a crisis, and as the population in Hong Kong edged past two million, the government closed the border. Refugees already on Hong Kong soil were to be deemed permanent residents, and future hopefuls would be turned away. This, however, did not stop the flow of refugees; people continued to cross the border illegally, in the next two to three decades, risking their lives.

The post-war baby boom and the refugees from China increased the population of Hong Kong by about one million each decade from the 1950s to the 1980s, putting severe stress on housing. Some landlords ingeniously divided tenement houses into cubicles. Others rented out bunk space where family members slept in shifts. Settlements of makeshift huts sprouted on the hillsides. By 1949, there were 300,000 squatter huts on Hong Kong Island and in Kowloon. Cooking fires, blazing right next to debris from the shacks, were an enormous fire hazard.[6] Overcrowding, lack of clean water, and malnutrition encouraged the transmission of many communicable diseases. Added to the problem was the Korean War, which broke out in 1950 and led to the embargo imposed on China and North Korea by the United Nations, shattering Hong Kong's recovering fragile trade status as an entrepôt, or port city. Entrepreneurial immigrants brought in capital and technology, however, while refugees provided a seemingly endless supply of cheap labour. Within a few years Hong Kong emerged as a major manufacturing centre.[7]

It was during the relentless years of post–Second World War poverty in Hong Kong that Rosie began her medical training. She saw first-hand the congestion and overcrowding in clinics and hospitals and many patients who could not afford to take time off from work to consult a doctor until they were gravely ill. Her experience no doubt inspired her commitment to public service in medicine.

The medical course at HKU then was six years. The curriculum for first year consisted of chemistry, physics, and biology. Classes were taught in Northcote Science Building, which had been newly erected before the war but had been demolished and replaced by another building since then. When lectures began in September 1946, students had to bring their own

---

6. Robin Hutcheon, *Highrise Society: The First Ten Years of Hong Kong Housing Society* (Hong Kong: Chinese University of Hong Kong Press, 1998), 3–4.
7. Tsang, *A Modern History of Hong Kong*, 162–67.

chairs or stools from home and carry them from room to room.[8] Luckily, by the time Rosie began her studies, permanent seats had become available. Rosie had not studied science subjects, but she loved mathematics and therefore had no problem with physics and chemistry. At the end of the academic year, although she did well in physics and chemistry, especially the latter, she failed biology—a serious blow. Unless she succeeded in a supplementary examination, she would lose her scholarship and have to repeat Year 1. That summer, she practised dissecting as many cockroaches, frogs, rats, and dogfish as she could find. When university began in the fall, she passed her supplementary examination with no difficulty.

The second year was a turning point for Rosie. Her lectures and laboratory work were mainly at the School of Anatomy and Physiology, just outside the western gate of the main campus. She had excellent teachers: physiology professor Lindsay Ride from Australia and anatomy professor Stanley Martin Banfill from Montreal.

Figure 2.3: The Northcote Science Building, circa 1950. Source: HKU Archives.

---

8. Bernard Mellor, *The University of Hong Kong: An Informal History* (Hong Kong: Hong Kong University Press, 1981), 111.

Lindsay Ride had been appointed professor of physiology at HKU in 1928. He was strongly in favour of HKU playing a bigger role in East Asia rather than serving just Hong Kong. When the university was in financial trouble during the 1930s, he argued strongly for keeping the clinical departments rather than leaving clinical teaching to volunteer private practitioners.[9] During the war, Professor Ride served in the British Army defending Hong Kong and was taken prisoner, but he escaped to Free China. From there, he obtained permission from the British military authority, MI9, to create the British Army Aid Group (BAAG), which under his command aided in the liberation of Hong Kong. BAAG escorted an estimated 800 Chinese political figures, non-Chinese soldiers and civilians, and 100 British soldiers, American Air Force personnel, and Indian soldiers to Free China.[10] Professor Ride was made a Commander of the Order of the British Empire (CBE MIL) in 1944 and received an Efficiency Decoration (ED) in 1948. After the war, Professor Ride helped restore HKU and became vice-chancellor in 1949.[11] He remembered the

Figure 2.4: Professor Lindsay Ride. Source: HKU Archives.

---

9. Lindsay Ride, 'Medical Education in Hong Kong', *Caduceus* 15, no. 4 (1936): 159–71.
10. Chan Sui-jeung, *East River Column: Hong Kong Guerillas in the Second World War and After* (Hong Kong: Hong Kong University Press, 2009), 49.
11. 'Sir Lindsay Ride C.B.E., Ed., M.A., D.M', *British Medical Journal* 2, no. 6096 (1977): 1228.

Yeung brothers before the war, and Rosie found him a devoted and effective teacher.

Dr Stanley Banfill, a Canadian army surgeon from Montreal, had been sent out to defend Hong Kong during the Japanese invasion. He was captured by Japanese soldiers, who were ready to kill him, but he pretended to be dead and rolled down a hill. Later he was caught again and was sent to Shamshuipo Camp and Argyle Street Camp between 1943 and 1945 as a prisoner of war, where he became one of the doctors in the camps and treated patients with great difficulty, because of shortage of medical supplies, drugs, and food. Yet he saved many lives and was awarded Member of the Order of the British Empire (MBE) in 1946.[12] While at the camp, Banfill studied anatomy, and he became professor of anatomy at HKU after the war. Rosie found him gentle yet firm.[13] During the weekly viva in anatomy, she invariably received a gold star. Banfill could not believe that the young woman who had failed first-year biology could do so well in anatomy, but he and Rosie's fellow students soon discovered that she had a photographic memory. She could remember the position of all the organs and structures during dissection.

These two devoted and excellent teachers, Professors Banfill and Ride, stimulated her interest in the subjects they taught, anatomy and physiology. In her second bachelor of medicine and bachelor of surgery (MBBS) examination, Rosie obtained distinctions in these two subjects.[14] They were excellent models for her as a teacher when she joined the university at a later date.

---

12. Hong Kong Veterans Commemorative Association. *Individual Report*. X03 Stanley Banfill, the Royal Canadian Army Medical Corps, accessed 16 February 2023, https://www.hkvca.ca/cforcedata/indivreport/indivdetailed.php?regtno=X03.
13. Kate Whitehead, 'Rosie Young, HKU Medic 1953', in *Confessions and Professions: Grand Rounds in Hong Kong Medicine*, ed. Madeline Slavick and Anna Koor (Hong Kong: MCCM Creations, 2019), 25.
14. The second MB examination was taken after the completion of the three courses, anatomy, physiology, and biochemistry, usually around the middle of the third year. Those who passed this examination would go on to three months of bedside teaching, when the techniques of history taking and clinical examination would be taught before they moved on to clinical years.

Figure 2.5: Professor S. M. Banfill. Source: HKU Archives.

The anatomy dissection laboratory, located on the ground floor of the School of Anatomy and Physiology, was a big room with a number of tables. On each table lay a cadaver, covered up completely. Once the cover was removed, students were hit by the pungent smell of chemicals used for preservation. Some found the odour nauseating. A few might faint during the first session, young men and women alike. Each cadaver was shared by six students, three on each side of the table. Three students on each side would dissect an arm and a leg, the head and the body shared by all six. Since they always worked together on the same cadaver for almost two years and learned to share and collaborate with each other, they became lifelong friends.[15]

Of the 120 students who entered medicine that year with Rosie, about 20 per cent were young women. Only forty students, or 30 per cent in total, made it all the way through. It was easy to be admitted to HKU Medical School, but it was difficult to graduate. Students who failed two of the three subjects in the first or second MBBS examinations were asked to leave.[16] Many had to repeat their last year when they failed the

---

15. Whitehead, 'Rosie Young, HKU Medic 1953', 25.
16. The first MBBS examination was after the first year at the completion of the courses in biology, organic chemistry, and physics.

final examination, and a few students took as long as ten years to obtain a medical degree. In 1953–1954, the medical curriculum was changed from six years to five years, when an upper six form (Secondary 7) was created in secondary schools to offer biology, chemistry, and physics at the first-year university level. The Faculty of Medicine's admission criteria became more stringent after that. The first-year medical class was smaller, usually around fifty students, but a higher percentage graduated.

Clinical Years

After the war, due to a greater number of students, the policy that all students must live in residence at HKU could no longer be implemented. Rosie lived at home for the first three years. Lady Ho Tung Hall, the only hall for women students at that time, was built with donations from Sir Robert Hotung in memory of his wife, Lady Margaret Hotung.[17] When the hall was opened in 1951, it had only eighty-five spaces. Rosie, entering the fourth year, was selected for one of them. She had earned a scholarship that covered her fees for both tuition and residence.

Due to the high tuition and boarding fee, most university students in those days came from an affluent background. In Lady Ho Tung Hall, the resident 'ladies' lived under the attentive care of the warden and hall attendants. They enjoyed three nutritious meals a day as well as laundry and room service. Dr Mary Ellison, wife of Professor Gordon King, was the first warden of Lady Ho Tung Hall. A stern matriarch, she maintained strict discipline. After roll call at 10 p.m., no one could enter the building unless permission had been sought ahead of time. Students were required to dress for dinner and to adhere to rules of etiquette. No one could leave the table until everyone had finished their meal. Servants stood at attention behind each table, ready to serve the students at any time. Because Rosie ate very quickly, she carried a book and read it below the dinner table after she completed her meal.[18] Dr Ellison, an obstetrician and gynaecologist like her husband, was concerned about anaemia, so once

---

17. Lady Ho Tung Hall, Hong Kong University, accessed 16 September 2022, http://www.hotung.hku.hk/.
18. Whitehead, 'Rosie Young, HKU Medic 1953', 26–27.

a week cow's liver, which Rosie detested, was served. Each young woman also received a bottle of milk at breakfast. Since Rosie disliked milk, she usually left her bottle for the resident in the next room.

Rosie enjoyed her clinical years. Lectures were held both at the main campus where the School of Pathology was, and at the Queen Mary Hospital at Pokfulam, some distance away. Those with a car sometimes offered free rides to fellow students, but occasionally others would charge for the ride. Medical students living at Lady Ho Tung Hall got a ride in the morning to the hospital from Professor Gordon King. His passengers both marvelled at and feared King's remarkable skill at driving backwards as fast as he drove forwards.

Many teachers in her clinical years impressed Rosie. Professor Hou Pao Chang, an internationally recognized pioneer in pathology, became HKU's first professor of pathology in the post-war years (1948–1960). He rebuilt from scratch the Pathology Department, which had been looted clean after the war. Professor Hou's research interests were broad, including cirrhosis of the liver, primary liver cancer, nasopharyngeal carcinoma, 'black fever', and others. It was the discovery of the relationship between the infestation of *Clonorchis sinensis* and biliary cirrhosis and primary carcinoma of the liver that pushed him to the forefront of cancer research. He demonstrated that infestation of parasites could lead to cirrhosis and then cancer—a novel hypothesis at the time.[19] He was also an expert in the history of Chinese medicine, applying his deep understanding of Western medicine to the historical investigation of Chinese medicine.[20] In his book *Science and Civilization in China*, Joseph Needham referred to Professor Hou as 'a pathologist and historian of anatomy and medicine'.[21]

---

19. Roy Cameron, *Hou Pao Chang: Biliary Cirrhosis* (Edinburgh: Oliver and Boyd, 1962), quoted in Ka-wai Fan, 'Pao-chang Hou (1893–1967): Pathologist and Historian of Chinese Medicine', *Journal of Medical Biography* 14, no. 4 (2006): 209.
20. Pao-Chang Hou, 'A History of Anatomy in China Yixye shi yu baojian zuzhi', *History of Medicine and Hygiene Organization* 1, no. 1 (1957): 64–73; quoted in Fan, 'Pao-chang Hou (1893–1967)', 209.
21. Joseph Needham, *Science and Civilization in China: Vol. 1* (Cambridge: Cambridge University Press, 1954), 12, quoted in Ka-wai Fan, 'Pao-chang Hou (1893–1967)', 209.

Professor Hou was a connoisseur of arts, calligraphy, and painting and had a deep respect for Chinese culture. In Chengdu, he visited old curio shops and stores of old books and collected many valuable items. He did the same in Hong Kong and bought the artefacts with any spare money he had, to prevent losing these precious items to overseas buyers. On his return to China, he donated his entire collection to the Palace Museum, consisting of 804 paintings, 506 ceramic works, and 2,067 books, all precious objects.[22]

After she graduated, Rosie would collaborate with him on research projects on biliary cirrhosis and liver cancer. She said that Professor Hou focused on teaching principles and not details. She respected him greatly for his professionalism and his originality in research.[23]

The celebrated author Han Suyin, a physician trained in the United Kingdom, lived in Hong Kong in the late 1940s and early 1950s, working as an assistant to Professor Hou and later as a medical officer in the hospital's Accident and Emergency Department. During the rare breaks in this period, she could be seen scribbling away at her desk in what would become the famous novel *A Many-Splendoured Thing*. Like Professor Hou, Han Suyin was a patriot, waiting in Hong Kong for the opportunity to return to serve her homeland.[24] On his retirement in 1960, Professor Hou returned to his alma mater, Peking Union Medical College (PUMC), and served there until his death in 1967.

Dr C. T. Huang, who later became the founding professor and chair of the HKU Department of Microbiology, taught Rosie during the time

---

22. 劉智鵬、劉蜀永,《侯寶璋家族史》(香港:和平圖書有限公司,2012),55–56.
23. 劉智鵬、劉蜀永,《侯寶璋家族史》,55–56.
24. Suyin Han, *My House Has Two Doors* (New York: Putnam, 1980), 36. She wrote: 'Prof Hou had come from China which made understanding of our similar hesitancies, dilemmas, and self-questioning immediate and our relations excellent. He too was waiting for the dust to settle. We both hated colonial subjugation, but we were also products of this subjugation, and in this duality became supple, flexible, knowing our quandary not havoc . . . neither he nor I were guilt-complex ridden, despite our respective Christian upbringings. We accepted ourselves, tolerating well the perpetual discomfort of being never entirely right, never entirely true, but in our imperfect way entire and flawless in our faith to our only religion, China.'

Figure 2.6: Professor Hou Pao Chang (sitting, centre), Dr C. T. Huang (sitting, first from the left), Dr Han Suyin (sitting, second from the left), and other staff of the Pathology Department, circa 1950. Source: Hong Kong Museum Medical Sciences.

when microbiology was part of the Pathology Department. Dr Huang had known Rosie's second brother, Woon Lam, when they both were at Jiangxi Medical School. From Dr Huang, Rosie learned about the life of her second brother when he was at Jiangxi Medical School, for which she was most grateful. They became good friends after she graduated.[25]

Most medical students had no idea which branch of medicine they wanted to enter after graduation, but Rosie did. Once she started attending the lectures of Professor A. J. S. McFadzean, her fate was sealed. She adored this handsome professor with a thick Scottish accent. McFadzean arrived in Hong Kong in 1948 and was the first post-war professor of medicine at HKU. He graduated from Glasgow University with honours as the

---

25. Whitehead, 'Rosie Young, HKU Medic 1953', 27.

most outstanding student of the year. In 1936, he volunteered for service with the Royal Army Medical Corps during the Second World War. After the war, he served as senior lecturer in the Muirhead Department of Medicine, Glasgow University, before his appointment at HKU.[26] His lectures inspired Rosie and the rest of her class. Like his colleague Professor Hou Pao Chang, Professor McFadzean discouraged rote learning and encouraged students to work out problems from first principles.

Rosie passed the final examination with distinction in medicine and was awarded the C. P. Fong Gold Medal in Medicine. For her required internship, she spent six months in internal medicine at HKU's University Medical Unit (UMU) at Queen Mary Hospital and six months at Tsan Yuk Hospital, a hospital for training in obstetrics and gynaecology.

Postgraduate Training

Once her internship was complete, Rosie joined UMU at Queen Mary Hospital for training in internal medicine under Professor McFadzean. Professor McFadzean, nicknamed Old Mac, was both respected and feared. There were many stories about Old Mac's Thursday morning clinics for teaching both staff and students. Most students arrived early to sit in the back row to escape being called upon to answer his questions. That left the first two rows of seats relatively empty. However, no place was safe. Dozing students would be hit by a flying piece of chalk (a common practice among teachers for dealing with dozing students at the time). Although McFadzean was fierce during teaching sessions, students knew him as the kindest of all the examiners.[27] He was a remarkable clinician, and his clinical acumen and knowledge were legendary. He emphasized

---

26. 'Obituary. A. J. S. McFadzean, OBE, DSc, MD, FRCP, FRCP Ed, FACP', *British Medical Journal* 6 (1974): 723.
27. Y. L. Yu, abridged version of the talk given by Prof Sir David Todd at the Inauguration of the Medical History Interest Group Held at the Hong Kong Museum of Medical Sciences on 17 January 2009. 'Reminiscences of Three Former Teachers: Prof AJS McFadzean, Dr Stephen Chang and Prof Gerald Choa', *Hong Kong Medical Journal* 15, no. 4 (2009): 315–19.

STUDENT DAYS   41

Figure 2.7: Rosie's graduation, MBBS degree, 1953.

Figure 2.8:   Queen Mary Hospital. Source: HKU Archives.

Figure 2.9: Professor A. J. S. McFadzean. Source: Department of Medicine, HKU.

the value of a detailed history and a good physical examination, counter to the current emphasis on laboratory investigations and imaging.

Three teams were responsible for the clinical care of patients at UMU. Each had a physician in charge, a trainee (clinical assistant or resident), and two house physicians (interns). Professor McFadzean led the first team, Dr Stephen Chang the second, and Dr Gerald Choa the third. Dr Chang was a graduate of the world-renowned Peking Union Medical College (PUMC). After receiving postgraduate training in Boston, specializing in infectious diseases, he became professor of medicine at Cheeloo University, arriving in Hong Kong after the war. Chang was an eminent clinician and teacher. Rosie found his lectures fascinating, and she remembered them for a long time afterwards. Highly approachable, Dr Chang was popular among students and trainees. In 1972, he moved to Nethersole Hospital, which was built by funds donated by the London Missionary Society and Dr Ho Kai in 1887, to head the Medical Department.

Dr Gerald Choa was the physician in charge on the ward where Rosie worked as a clinical assistant. Choa was a devout Catholic. In addition to mentoring her in medicine, he looked after Rosie's spiritual health and ensured that she went to church every Sunday. Rosie was converted to the

Figure 2.10: Dr Stephen Chang (left) and Dr Gerald Choa (right). Source: Department of Medicine, HKU.

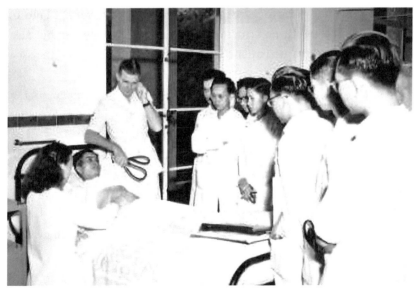

Figure 2.11: Professor McFadzean, bedside teaching, 1951. Source: Department of Medicine, HKU.

Catholic faith in the summer of 1951 and attended the chapel at Ricci Hall regularly. At that time, the Catholic doctors in Hong Kong were establishing the Guild of St Luke, St Cosmas, and St Damian. At Dr Choa's request, Rosie became a founding member. Dr Choa was a superb clinician and an erudite teacher, particularly in cardiology and neurology. Impeccably dressed, he was very much a gentleman physician.[28] Dr Choa would leave UMU in 1956 to become the specialist in the government Medical and Health Service. In 1970, he was appointed director of the Medical and Health Department—an important position that permitted him to serve the population in Hong Kong in a completely different capacity. After retirement from government service, Dr Choa became the founding dean of the Faculty of Medicine at the Chinese University of Hong Kong.

Rosie's fourth memorable clinical teacher was Dr C. P. Fong, who, like her brother Woon Lam, had attended Jiangxi Medical School. He shared stories with Rosie about her brother and the lives of the other medical students there. A brilliant teacher, Dr Fong once delivered a lecture on behalf of Professor McFadzean, without preparation. He would spend hours by the bedside of a patient who had refused surgery, trying to convince him of the necessity of the procedure. Few doctors would have that kind of patience, and Rosie learned from him not only clinical acumen but also how to treat patients with patience and kindness, no matter how busy she was.

Under the tutelage of these four superb clinicians, Rosie could not but become an astute and compassionate clinician and an excellent teacher herself.

During the depressed economy of the late 1940s and early 1950s, the Hong Kong government wisely concentrated its meagre resources on the control and prevention of infectious diseases rather than on curative care. As a result, few new hospitals were built, and the existing hospitals were always overcrowded. At Queen Mary Hospital, this meant placing camp beds between regular beds and on the veranda. In other hospitals, it was

---

28. Yu, 'Reminiscences of Three Former Teachers', 315–19.

not uncommon for two patients to share a bed.[29] To help relieve the situation, the Hong Kong government encouraged non-governmental agencies such as missionary societies to build and operate clinics and hospitals.

During the immediate post-war years, epidemics of infectious diseases were frequent because of severe overcrowded housing, water shortage, poor sanitation, poverty, and malnutrition. Tuberculosis, smallpox, cholera, and typhoid claimed many lives. As at other hospitals, the medical wards at Queen Mary Hospital were filled with patients suffering from infections or from infectious or parasitic diseases, such as pneumonia, bacillary or amoebic dysentery, fever from a variety of causes, including malaria and subacute bacterial endocarditis, and jaundice due to recurrent pyogenic cholangitis. There were patients with chronic rheumatic heart disease with different types of heart murmurs, haematemesis due to peptic ulcer or oesophageal varices, hepatomegaly due to primary cancer of the liver, and splenomegaly due to cryptogenic cirrhosis of the liver. Many of these diseases have now disappeared from hospital wards, mostly due to effective prevention, but at that time their pathogenesis was still poorly understood. The diagnosis usually came too late, and treatment was either unavailable or ineffective.

Each ward at Queen Mary Hospital had twenty to twenty-five beds. Because verandas and the space between beds were filled with makeshift camp beds, the total capacity per ward could reach thirty-five. UMU had five general wards under its jurisdiction in the early 1950s. The five wards took turns admitting emergency patients. At times more than ten patients could be admitted in twenty-four hours.

The life of an intern in those days was far from the glamorous portrayal presented in the 1969–1970 British television series *Doctor in the House*.[30] The Hong Kong government had no funds for twenty-four-hour laboratory services in hospitals. It was the duty of the interns to carry out blood counts and examine urine for blood, protein, and cells, stool for

---

29. Robin Hutcheon, *Bedside Manners: Hospital and Health Care in Hong Kong* (Hong Kong: Chinese University of Hong Kong Press, 1999), 35.
30. *Doctor in the House* was a popular British television comedy series based on a set of books and a film of the same name by Richard Gordon in 1969 and 1970.

occult blood and parasitic ova when indicated on admission, as well as obtaining clinical histories and conducting physical examinations. The poor interns were expected to complete everything, including laboratory investigations, and have patients started on appropriate treatment before the next morning rounds with their seniors. It was not uncommon for interns to get no sleep and carry on as usual on the following day. One of the intern's responsibilities was catching microfilaria, which inconveniently appear only at midnight in the blood in patients with filariasis. The other unenviable task was examining, by a patient's bedside, for crawling amebae on a microscopic slide that had been prepared by smearing a very fresh specimen of stool. All interns and trainees acquired laboratory skills that turned out to be very useful for research work in their future careers.

Ward rounds and any orders regarding sick patients had to be completed before the interns who were not on call could leave the hospital on Sundays. There was no annual leave. This sort of life would generate strong protests these days, but at the time, there were no complaints. It was considered a privilege to be admitted and to graduate from the Faculty of Medicine, and the very sick patients who were brought to the hospital had to be looked after despite the staff shortage. Midnight snacks of delicious prawn congee from the nearby restaurants, laughter and jokes, all helped to relieve the stress, and there was an esprit de corps among the interns and residents that is no longer common. The stories of Old Mac and various patients became memories that people treasured and reminisced about whenever they met in later years.

Infected with the Research Bug

Research was in Professor McFadzean's blood. While at the University of Glasgow he became interested in haematology, publishing original papers in the field. He continued to pursue this interest after he arrived in Hong Kong and developed others, particularly clinical questions about prevalent local diseases. His research was wide-ranging, including diseases of the liver, thyroid, spleen, and blood, and his intellectual curiosity was contagious. Before long, all members of his department were engaged in research,[31] some of which led to the cure or prevention of some local diseases and was partly responsible for their gradual disappearance. Professor McFadzean strongly believed that teaching, research, and clinical service must go hand in hand, and he stressed the importance of research to clinical practice. Rosie's training was like that of any other trainee. During her first year as a resident, she helped her seniors with their projects, but soon she conceived her own research question and project.

At that time many patients suffered from primary cancer of the liver, and a few of them developed hypoglycaemic attacks. Since these patients were not diabetic and not taking insulin, the question of why they had these attacks became Rosie's research project and her Doctor of Medicine (MD) thesis. On Sunday mornings, Old Mac usually invited Rosie into his office after clinical rounds or church. She would prepare a fresh cup of coffee for him, and then a tutorial on her research project began. Old Mac would review the progress of her research during the previous week, discuss with her the significance of her findings, and suggest what to do as the next step. By the end of three years, she had her MD thesis, entitled 'Carbohydrate Metabolism in Hepatocellular Carcinoma', written up and submitted. Rosie had a very special relationship with Old Mac, whom she regarded as her second father. In later years, she cared for him whenever he was ill.

The year 1958 brought both personal honours and losses to Rosie. She obtained her MD degree and was awarded a Sino-British Trust Scholarship for postgraduate studies overseas. Sadly, however, she lost her mother from cerebral haemorrhage due to hypertension, and her older brother, Wai Lam, from colon cancer, at the young age of forty-three. It was a terrible blow to lose two family members within six months. Rosie channelled her thoughts and energy into preparing for her move to Glasgow for further studies at the hospital where her mentor had trained. There she would be supervised by Old Mac's own former teacher. Old

---

31. David Todd, 'Tribute', in *Centenary Tribute to Professor AJS McFadzean: A Legacy for Medicine in Hong Kong* (Hong Kong: Hong Kong Academy of Medicine Press, 2015), 8–9.

Figure 2.12: Rosie's MD diploma, 1959.

Figure 2.13: Rosie (sitting, first from the left) with several other MDs in the Faculty of Medicine, at the university's Golden Jubilee Celebration, 1961. Source: Department of Medicine, HKU.

Mac wanted her to have the best of training and to be looked after while she was in Glasgow.

Because of these recent losses, her father insisted that Rosie travel by sea to Glasgow. Air travel was not as safe then as it is today. The boat stopped briefly at a few major ports, allowing her to disembark for sightseeing. The excitement of experiencing different cultures proved to be an excellent distraction. When she arrived in London, Rosie was met at the airport by someone from the Sino-British Trust. She stayed with a family in London for a few days before continuing her journey to Glasgow.

The trust had arranged for Rosie to live in a student residence close to the Glasgow Royal Infirmary. As the residence did not provide meals, she ate regularly at the hospital. The change of diet to bread and potatoes, the cold weather that encouraged a good appetite, and the physical inactivity while she studied for her professional examinations all contributed to the rare gain of twenty pounds. Rosie had always been petite and slender, so her weight gain necessitated a completely new wardrobe. By the time she returned to Hong Kong, however, most of the additional weight had disappeared.

As expected, Rosie passed on her first attempt the professional examinations of both the Royal College of Physicians of London, which earned her the status of a specialist in internal medicine, and the Royal College of Physicians of Edinburgh, which gave her the status of a specialist in haematology. Once the examinations were over, she immediately changed her focus to another specialty—endocrinology. She realized during her training that two senior colleagues in the same department had already been fully trained in haematology. That meant she would be 'the little third' in haematology at Queen Mary Hospital, always taking a back seat to her two seniors. Also, patients with blood disorders were not common enough to require four specialists (Old Mac was a haematologist) in the same department at the same hospital. It would be very difficult for Rosie to get promoted in that field since promotion at HKU depended on a vacancy. Endocrinology was going through a golden era at the time because new drugs for treating thyroid diseases and diabetes and new methods of hormone measurement were being discovered. Rosie felt that the work was like being a detective, requiring investigations that were logical and step by step. Dr Gerald Choa was interested in patients with diabetes and thyrotoxicosis, and he had advised Rosie that this might be a fruitful area for future research. Moreover, she did not like invasive procedures or being roused in the middle of the night by calls from patients, as in cardiology. While in Glasgow, Rosie started attending rounds and talks on endocrinology. Before she headed home, she spent a month at the Postgraduate Medical School at Hammersmith Hospital in London, to learn more about the field.

What impressed her most during her sabbatical year was the kindness of the people in Glasgow. On several occasions, ladies offered help when Rosie appeared to be lost, taking her to the bus stop and asking the bus driver to make sure that this young girl would get off at the right stop. Rosie has always looked younger than her age. One weekend, when Rosie was returning from Edinburgh to Glasgow, her train arrived later than expected. She found herself the only one in an empty train station at around 11:00 p.m. The buses had stopped running and there were no taxis around. As she was hesitating over walking to the Royal Infirmary about twenty minutes away, a man came slowly towards her and politely asked her if he could accompany her to her residence. He smelled of alcohol, but on a quick assessment Rosie could see he was not stumbling or swaying. During the short walk, he kept his distance. When they arrived at the hospital, the man bowed slightly to her and took his leave. Rosie returned to Hong Kong to enter the next stage of her career, but she would always remember the warm-heartedness of the Glaswegians.

During her university and postgraduate training days, Rosie had several excellent mentors whom she emulated. She matured into a highly skilled and empathetic clinician who cared for the well-being of her patients and a devoted and tireless teacher and mentor.

Plate 1: Professor Young at her alma mater during graduation day, circa 1996.

Plate 2: Professor Young teaching the basic physician training course in the 1980s.
Source: Department of Medicine, HKU.

Plate 3: Endocrinology and Metabolic Diseases Unit, Professor Young (sitting, right), and Professor Karen Lam (sitting, left), 1985. Source: Department of Medicine, HKU.

Plate 4: MRCP Celebration dinner in Hong Kong in the 1980s. Professor Young (centre, left), and Professor David Todd (centre, right). Source: Department of Medicine, HKU.

Plate 5: Department of Medicine, HKU, Professor Young (sitting, second from the right) Professor David Todd (sitting, centre), 1985. Source: Department of Medicine, HKU.

Plate 6: Professor Young teaching in 2017. Source: Department of Medicine, HKU.

Plate 7: Professor Young's 90th birthday celebration, October 2020. Source: Department of Medicine, HKU.

Plate 8: Professor Young auctioning, raising funds for the HKU Foundation, 2019. Source: Department of Medicine, HKU.

Plate 9: Professor Gerald Choa, founding dean of the Faculty of Medicine, CUHK. Source: Faculty of Medicine, CUHK.

Plate 10: Professor Young, pro-vice-chancellor (left), and Professor Rayson Huang, vice-chancellor (right), after Dr Pauline Chan (centre) received an LLD (Hon) from HKU, 1985.

Plate 11: The 120th anniversary celebration dinner, HKU Faculty of Medicine, 2007. Source: Department of Medicine, HKU.

Plate 12: Professor Young (front, sixth from the left), at the Big Shots Photograph Exhibition, part of the 130th anniversary celebration, HKU Faculty of Medicine, 2017. Source: Faculty of Medicine, HKU.

Plate 13: Professor Young passing the torch, at the homecoming dinner of the 130th anniversary celebration, HKU Faculty of Medicine, 2017. Source: Faculty of Medicine, HKU.

Plate 14: Professor Young (seventh from the right), at the homecoming dinner of the 130th anniversary celebration, HKU Faculty of Medicine, 2017. 'Those Were the Days' and 'Here's to the Future' (the word 'Future' was not captured in the photo) are the handwriting of Professor Sir David Todd, who passed away earlier that year. Source: Faculty of Medicine, HKU.

Plate 15: Current and former staff of the Department of Medicine, celebrating the 130th anniversary of Faculty of Medicine, 2017. Source: Department of Medicine, HKU.

Plate 16: Professor Young (centre, left) and Dean Gabriel Leung (centre, right), at the HKU Medical Alumni Association Meeting in Victoria, Australia, August 2018. Source: Faculty of Medicine, HKU.

Plate 17: The 2018 white coat ceremony of the Faculty of Medicine HKU and orientation of first-year students, presided over by Professor Young (sitting, with a bouquet), Dean Gabriel Leung on her right, with other members of the Faculty of Medicine and first-year students. Source: Faculty of Medicine, HKU.

Plate 18: Professor Young (left), Dr the Honourable Sir David Li Kwok Po (centre), and Professor Arthur Li (right), after Professor Young's Honorary University Fellowship Award Ceremony, 2019. Source: Department of Medicine, HKU.

Plate 19: Professor Young (sixth from the right) at the Primary Healthcare Blueprint Symposium, 15 January 2023.

Plate 20: Hospital Authority Board, Sir S. Y. Chung (sitting, centre), Professor Young (standing, sixth from the right), 1995.

Plate 21: The SARS Expert Committee, Chief Executive Tung Chee-hwa (front, fourth from the left), Professor Young (front, second from the left), 2003.

Plate 22: Professor Young visiting the Chinese Foundation Secondary School with Dr Sophia Chan, 2019.

Plate 23: Professor Young awarded a DSc (*honoris causa*) from HKU, 1995.

Plate 24: From left: Professor Rayson Huang, Professor Rosie Young, Lady Young, and Sir L. T. Young after Professor Rosie Young's DSc (HKU) Award Ceremony, 1995.

Plate 25: Professor Young awarded Honorary University Fellowship from HKU, 2019. Source: Department of Medicine, HKU.

Plate 26: Professor Young, awarded the Grand Bauhinia Medal from Chief Executive Carrie Lam, 2018.

3

An Academic in Medicine

A Physician at the University Medical Unit

Hong Kong's economy continued to expand as the city transformed into a major manufacturing centre. The high economic growth was sustained into the early 1980s. Socio-economic factors determined not only medical developments but also the epidemiology of diseases in Hong Kong. Although infectious diseases and infection were the major causes of death during the first post-war decade, that changed with the availability of antibiotics, better nutrition due to a higher standard of living, and effective control and prevention by the Medical and Health Department. As the economy advanced, people in Hong Kong adopted a Western style of living and a Western diet. By the early 1970s, noncommunicable diseases, such as cancer, coronary heart disease, stroke, and diabetes, had taken over the medical scene, and they remain the major causes of death.

The meagre budget allocated for the Medical and Health Department in the late 1940s and early 1950s gave way to a less stringent one in subsequent decades. In 1964, the government published a White Paper on the future development of medical services in Hong Kong.[1] The report

---

1. Hong Kong Government, *Development of Medical Services in Hong Kong* (Hong Kong: Government Printers, 1964).

recommended that medical services be increased in the next ten years—to provide outpatient care for the 50 per cent of the population that could not afford to see private general practitioners, and in-patient care for the 80 per cent of the population who could not afford hospital services. Accordingly, a huge building programme of more hospitals and clinics dominated the following two decades, including more facilities for training medical students.

In 1959, there were only 0.36 doctors/1,000 population in Hong Kong, compared to the 2.5/1,000 ratio recommended by the World Health Organization for developing countries. Of 700 positions in the Medical and Health Department, more than 100 were unfilled. The government made an urgent request that HKU increase medical student enrolment by one-third, granting the university a subsidy with guaranteed increases over the next seven years. For the first time in its history, the university could embark on a programme of expansion—a cause for celebration on the occasion of its Golden Jubilee in 1961.[2] Medical enrolment would continue to expand in the following two decades.

It was during this period of great expansion that Rosie returned to her alma mater to begin her career in academic medicine. She would go on to play a vital role in the development of medicine at HKU and in Hong Kong as a whole.

As a specialist, Rosie became one of the physicians in UMU at Queen Mary Hospital in 1960. The team she led was responsible for the patients in two hospital wards. Rosie conducted official rounds once a week, reviewing the status of every patient under her team's care with her juniors. A round usually took the whole morning, as it always involved teaching. Rosie was available for her team every day. UMU also provided consultation for other services in the hospital. There was a physician at UMU on the roster to provide this consultation and to be responsible for patients admitted during the evenings and at night. In that role, Rosie was known for her clinical acuity, her thoroughness, and her sense of responsibility.

---

2. Dafydd Emrys Evans, *Constancy of Purpose: An Account of the Foundation and History of Hong Kong College of Medicine and the Faculty of Medicine of the University of Hong Kong, 1887–1987* (Hong Kong: Hong Kong University Press, 1987), 87–100.

Rosie had learned a great deal from Professor McFadzean, not only in clinical skill but also from his attitude to patients. Professor McFadzean was devoted to his patients and would do all he could to help them. On one occasion, he wanted to admit to hospital a patient suffering from typhoid. Because the patient had no means of transportation, he drove her from her home to Queen Mary Hospital in his own car. As a result, he developed typhoid fever himself.

Rosie often returned to the wards in the evening, conducting an informal round and chatting with patients. One young patient had been admitted for treatment of complications related to tuberculosis. One evening she found him working hard on school assignments. Because his hospitalization was prolonged, he had brought his schoolbooks with him. An excellent student, the young patient wanted to be an engineer. From then on, Rosie helped him with mathematics. After he left the hospital, they lost touch. But just recently Rosie received a surprise call from him. The young patient had gone on to complete an engineering degree, then returned to university to read mathematics. At the time he contacted Rosie, he had just retired as a professor in mathematics at a university in the United States! His success, he told Rosie, had all been due to her stimulating tutorials.

Rosie enjoyed teaching students, a trait she has had since childhood. Clinical teaching took place at the bedside in small groups, giving students practical experience. For medicine and surgery, students were required to do three months of clerkship on the wards during the fourth and the fifth years (junior and senior clerkships). For obstetrics, students had to deliver at least twenty babies while living at Tsan Yuk Hospital for two months. Rosie especially enjoyed the evening rounds after dinner, when she would gather all the clinical clerks, interns, and residents who were not busy to discuss in detail one or two patients on the ward. Afterwards, the group might go out for a snack before heading home. For safety reasons, she always asked the young men to accompany the young women to their residence before returning to their own residence hall. Her after-hours teaching was something that students looked forward to, and Rosie was one of the most popular teachers at the time. Her students ranked her as one of the best teachers they had in the medical school.

During the late 1960s, medical wards in Hong Kong began to fill with patients suffering from heart attacks due to coronary heart diseases, stroke resulting from cerebrovascular diseases, pneumonias, and cancers rather than infectious diseases.[3] Professor McFadzean saw the epidemiological change in disease pattern in the UK in the 1950s with progressive improvement in economy and better diet. He had the foresight to send junior staff members for training overseas in various specialties, and these young men and women returned with new skills and knowledge. Gradually different teams (later called divisions) such as cardiology, haematology, neurology, gastroenterology, respiratory, nephrology, and rheumatology were established to serve patients.[4]

Shortly after she became a physician at UMU at Queen Mary Hospital, Rosie headed up the Endocrinology and Metabolic Diseases Unit (later Division), the first of its kind in Hong Kong, fully utilizing her leadership skills, which she developed during the war. During those years, she made vital decisions to keep the family from starving and from malnutrition, and to plan ahead. At Queen Mary Hospital, she was assigned some beds specifically for the management of patients with endocrine and metabolic disorders and established an outpatient clinic for these patients. In addition to the clinical unit, she set up a hormone laboratory and began her research. With the clinical and research facilities, though limited at the time, she began training young doctors who were interested in becoming subspecialists in this area and stimulated their interest in research. In time, the Endocrinology and Metabolic Disease Division at Queen Mary Hospital became the major referral centre in Hong Kong to provide a comprehensive range of services for diseases such as diabetes, thyroid, and lipids disorders.[5] In 1989, she initiated the KK Leung Diabetes Centre to provide ambulatory service, also the first of its kind in Hong Kong. It delivered a comprehensive service on diabetes care with on-site dietician consultation and facilities for patient education. Initially it was located

---

3. *Hong Kong Medical and Health Department Annual Reports*, 1961 and 1971.
4. Department of Medicine, *Achievements in Medicine, 1985–1995* (Hong Kong: The University of Hong Kong, 1995), 2.
5. *Department of Medicine (1993–2019): Impact, Inspirations* (Hong Kong: The University of Hong Kong, 2021), 135.

only at Queen Mary Hospital but later in Sai Ying Pun Outpatient Clinic too.⁶

Christina Wang, professor of medicine at Harbor-UCLA Medical Centre, succeeded her as head of the Endocrinology and Metabolic Diseases Division before she left for the US. She wrote: 'She [Professor Young] trained all the endocrinologists in the department and in the whole of Hong Kong when I was there [at UMU]. She is an excellent clinician and even today I am using her teachings in the management of patients and teaching the fellows and residents.'⁷

A Year at Cambridge

In July 1962, Rosie met Professor Frank Young from Cambridge University. Young had been invited to Hong Kong as a member of a commission chaired by Professor J. S. Fulton (the Fulton Commission) to investigate the possibility of establishing a second university in Hong Kong.

Rosie's meeting with Professor Frank Young, who had called on Professor McFadzean during his visit, ended with Rosie receiving an invitation to spend a year in the Department of Biochemistry at Cambridge University. She was also awarded a Smith and Nephew Research Fellowship to support her time there.

Rosie's year in Cambridge proved fruitful and intellectually stimulating. She learned new techniques to measure different hormones, using radioimmunoassay or biological or physiological methods. Any spare time she had was spent attending lectures and meetings at the university. She absorbed as much new information as she could while enjoying the atmosphere and the culture. Her visit was enriched by meeting a number of people who proved to be valuable to her career in later years. In 1988, she was made an Honorary Fellow, Newnham College, University of Cambridge.

During the time in Cambridge, Rosie called on Joseph Needham, professor of biochemistry, world-renowned not for the work in his field but

---

6. Personal communication with Professor Karen Lam by email on 14 July 2023.
7. Personal communication with Professor Christina Wang by email on 16 July 2023.

for his scientific research and writings on the history of Chinese science and technology. Needham's multivolume *Science and Civilisation in China* earned him many honours. Needham's residence in Cambridge was the focal point for gatherings of students from China. He organized buffet lunches or dinners during festivals and holidays for students. Labelled as a 'red' because of his objection to the Korean War, Needham was avoided by some of the local staff and students. Although cautioned not to do so, Rosie visited Needham several times, enjoying the occasions. She also visited museums and other interesting sites, and toured Europe during her time away.

The Research Years

After returning from her year in Cambridge, Rosie set up the equipment necessary to pursue her research in endocrinology and metabolic diseases. Over the next few years, Rosie would discover that hypoglycaemic attacks occurred not infrequently among patients with carcinoma of the liver and in patients with other types of liver disease, such as recurrent pyogenic cholangitis.[8] The symptoms of hypoglycaemia could be reversed completely with administration of glucose by mouth or intravenously, depending on the status of the patient. She also documented the occurrence of periodic paralysis in patients with thyrotoxicosis—a condition that occurred mainly in Chinese males during the summer months and between 9:00 p.m. and 9:00 a.m., precipitated by severe exercise and a high carbohydrate intake the previous evening. She discovered that the episodes of paralysis were due to low potassium in the blood and were relieved by potassium supplement.[9] Rosie defined the clinical features of this group of patients and outlined the possible causes of paralysis and its

---

8. A. J. S. McFadzean and T. T. Yeung, 'Hypoglycaemia in Suppurative Pancholangitis due to *Clonorchis sinensis*', *Transactions of the Royal Society of Tropical Medicine and Hygiene* 59 (1965): 179–81. Recurrent pyogenic cholangitis is a condition due to infection of the bile duct with stones and intrahepatic stones as a result of infestation by the liver fluke, *Clonorchis sinensis*.
9. A. J. S. McFadzean and T. T. Yeung, 'Periodic Paralysis Complicating Thyrotoxicosis in Chinese', *British Medical Journal* 1 (1967): 451–55.

prevention.[10] Since this condition occurred only among Chinese patients, it was likely to be genetically determined. The findings of these studies are not only important in the prevention and treatment of periodic paralysis in patients with thyrotoxicosis but further our understanding of carbohydrate metabolism in health and disease. All her discoveries stand the test of time and remain valid. Rosie also conducted investigations on many aspects of diabetes and endocrinology disorders in Hong Kong.[11]

This period turned out to be the most productive time in her research career. During her academic life, she would publish more than one hundred scientific papers in international journals. She loved the excitement of discovering a new syndrome, a new disease, a new method of treatment, or the newly discovered cause of a disease. She also enjoyed travelling to different places to present her new research findings at international conferences and to meet other researchers in the same field.

In 1968, Rosie was awarded the China Medical Board Fellowship to visit the Metabolic Research Unit at the Medical Centre of the University of California at San Francisco (UCSF) and the Department of Endocrinology, University of Michigan Medical School, Ann Arbor. Again, her father insisted that she travel by boat. Instead of going to San Francisco directly, she stopped off in Hawaii for a much-deserved and leisurely holiday visiting with her uncle's family, arriving in San Francisco almost one month later. On the university campus in San Francisco, she was greeted by long-haired young men and women in colourful attire, carrying banners and protesting against the Vietnam War. It was the era of student activism and sexual revolution.

In the Metabolic Research Unit at UCSF, Rosie spent about a month joining ward rounds, observing, and discussing various issues with researchers. She developed her own research question and set up equipment in a corner of one of the laboratories. She was ready to start on her project when a telegram arrived from Professor McFadzean informing

---

10. R. T. T. Yeung and T. F. Tse, 'Thyrotoxic Periodic Paralysis: Effect of Propranolol', *American Journal of Medicine* 57 (1974): 584–90.
11. R. T. T. Yeung, and L. K. F. Chan, 'A Study of Diabetes Mellitus and Its Complications among the Chinese of Hong Kong', *Philippine Journal of Internal Medicine* 13 (1975): 56–61.

her that her father was very ill. Rosie left San Francisco by air the following day. At the Hong Kong airport, she was met by Professor McFadzean and Dr David Todd, her senior colleague, who took her to the hospital. Fortunately, although her father was very sick, he responded to treatment. Rosie remained in Hong Kong to oversee her father's recovery, which took more than a month, and she did not return to San Francisco.

In the following year, 1969, Rosie decided to complete her China Medical Board Fellowship. She returned to the Medical Centre at UCSF for three months before proceeding to Professor J. W. Conn's endocrinology unit at the University of Michigan Medical School in Ann Arbor. Professor Conn had first reported what became known as Conn's syndrome in 1955 in a patient who had hypertension with an aldosterone-producing adenoma.[12] While in Ann Arbor, Rosie obtained a letter of introduction to visit the US National Institute of Health (NIH) in Bethesda, Maryland. While at NIH, she offered to give a talk on her research findings. Thinking back years later, Rosie wondered at her own bravery in suggesting she lecture at such a prestigious centre at the

Figure 3.1: Rosie, early 1970s.

---

12. Malvinder S. Parmar and Shikha Singh, 'Conn Syndrome', accessed 16 February 2023, https://www.ncbi.nlm.nih.gov/books/NBK459197/#:~:text=Conn%20syndrome%20was%20named%20after,renin%2C%20hypertension%2C%20and%20hypokalemia.

time—an act that was quite rash. She spent a final three months in the endocrinology unit at the University of Chicago, before returning to Hong Kong in 1970.

A Dilemma

Rosie had been appointed assistant lecturer at HKU before she left for her examinations. After receiving her professional qualification, she remained in the same position with the same pay. As noted, according to HKU regulations, no one could be promoted until there was a vacancy. There were also several unfair issues regarding Rosie's salary. First, it was only about 80 per cent of the salaries of her male counterparts, a practice following that in the civil service.[13] Female government employees had submitted numerous petitions to the government demanding equal pay, without success.[14] It was not until the early 1970s that this demand was met.[15] Second, doctors employed by the government received higher salaries than did their counterparts employed by the university even though university staff often worked harder, since research activities were usually carried out after working hours. As a result, the university had difficulty in recruiting talented young people. In the 1960s, Professor McFadzean negotiated directly with the government financial secretary to obtain equal pay for university medical personnel. Naturally, this won him the hearts and the respect of all university staff.[16] The third issue was that expatriates working for the government received free accommodation and an extra allowance, but the locals did not. Rosie, a Chinese female and a university medical

---

13. Colonial Secretariat, *Report on Women's Salary Scales in Public Service* (Hong Kong Government: Government Printer 1962), 1.
14. 'Petition by Doctors: Approach to Mr. Sandys for Equal Treatment', *South China Sunday Post*, 17 March 1963; 'Question About H.K. Women Doctors' Pay Raised in Lords: London', *South China Morning Post*, 9 April 1963, 10 April 1963.
15. 'Equal Pay for Women in Civil Services Proposed by 1975', *South China Morning Post*, 29 February 1968.
16. Y. L. Yu, 'Reminiscences of Three Former Teachers: Prof AJS McFadzean, Dr Stephan Chang and Prof Gerald Choa', *Hong Kong Medical Journal* 15, no. 4 (2009): 315–19.

staff, received about 50 per cent of the salary paid to a male expatriate doctor working in the government Medical and Health Department.

From time to time, Rosie thought about leaving the university for private practice because of the unfairness. That was especially true after the death of her older brother, Wai Lam, in 1958. Before Wai Lam passed away, he had asked Rosie to take over his private office and his popular practice. Her income would be much higher, and with the extra money she could help Wai Lam's young family after his death. The offer was very difficult for her to refuse for that reason. She sought advice from her father, who told her to follow the path that she had chosen and not to worry about the economic aspects, and that Wai Lam's family would be fine. Rosie loved her work at UMU: her academic career brought not wealth but meaning and satisfaction.

Life for Rosie was busy but enjoyable during these years, filled with exciting research, promising students, and interesting patients. On most weekdays, if she was not on call, she spent the evening teaching clinical clerks or conducting experiments in her laboratory. On Sunday mornings, after attending mass, Rosie had the usual stimulating discussions about her research findings over a cup of coffee with Old Mac. Sunday evenings she returned home to have dinner with her father and other members of her family. UMU at Queen Mary Hospital was her second home. As an employee of the university, she was not given accommodation at the hospital. To be close to her patients and her research laboratory, she often stayed with a female colleague, a government medical officer who was provided with accommodation in the hospital residence.

During the late 1960s and early 1970s, Old Mac's health deteriorated. His migraine attacks became more frequent. Rosie visited him at home to give him his medications and then sat by his bedside, holding his hand, until he fell asleep.

Rosie was petite, attractive, and lively, and she had no shortage of admirers, locally and overseas. So far, however, she had not encountered anyone who came close to her conception of an ideal partner—someone like her second brother, Woon Lam, whom she had idolized. Also, she enjoyed her work very much. Why give up her promising career for someone less than ideal?

Figure 3.2: Professor McFadzean and Rosie, 1974.

1974: A Year of Transition

The inevitable time arrived when Old Mac had to retire. Even though he loved Rosie like a daughter, regarded her abilities highly, and appreciated her dedication to the department and to him, he did not consider her for his successor. Instead, he nominated Dr David Todd as the next head of department, citing Dr Todd's administrative and political skills—skills that Rosie had not acquired at the time. Dr Todd was promoted to professor in 1972.

Rosie had known for a long time that she would not be considered for the position of department head. Not only was Professor Todd an astute clinician, a talented researcher with an analytical mind, a much-appreciated teacher, and her senior, he was also immensely popular with his colleagues. A few months before his retirement, Professor McFadzean asked both his beloved students into his office. He told them that he would be nominating Professor David Todd as the next head of the department and asked Rosie to help David in his new role to advance the department. In the decades to follow, she would support not only Professor Todd but all subsequent heads of the department. Professor Todd and others were highly appreciative of her assistance.

Before he left, however, Professor McFadzean fought to have Rosie promoted. He told the Faculty Promotion Committee that '[h]er promotion is long overdue! What else is there to assess!' Rosie became professor (personal chair) of medicine at HKU in 1974 without an interview, which was unheard of before that time. Thanks to the thriving economy and a larger budget for the university, two professorships within the same department became possible by then.

Professor A. J. S. McFadzean had served as dean of the Faculty of Medicine and vice-chancellor of the university during his tenure, and he greatly aided the expansion of the university and the faculty after the war. By the time he retired, he had successfully accomplished his two major missions: to educate and train local doctors to staff the health care system in Hong Kong and to pass on the chair to a local graduate.[17] His retirement ended an important era of medicine in Hong Kong.

A few months after Professor McFadzean's departure for Glasgow, sad news came that he had passed away in hospital there. Members of the medical circle in Hong Kong, almost all of them his trainees, mourned the loss of their former professor.

Under the administration of Professor Todd, with the able assistance of Professor Young, the Department of Medicine at HKU became known internationally as an excellent centre for clinical research and learning. Since 1985, the Royal College of Physicians examinations had been held

---

17. Richard Yu, ‚Preface‘, in *Centenary Tribute to Professor AJS McFadzean*, 7.

Figure 3.3: Department of Medicine, HKU, Professor McFadzean (sitting, centre), Professor David Todd (sitting, seventh from the left). Professor Rosie Young (sitting, fifth from the left), and members of the department, including honorary staff, 1974. Source: Department of Medicine, HKU.

Figure 3.4: Cocktail Reception in Hong Kong Country Club, Professor McFadzean (centre), Professor David Todd (third from the right), Professor Rosie Young (fifth from the left), 1974. Source: Department of Medicine, HKU.

in Hong Kong, so candidates no longer need to travel to the UK. In the 1980s, postgraduate training in Hong Kong was further formalized, with Professor Young serving as a member of the Government Working Party on Postgraduate Medical Education and Training. Professor Todd would go on to become the founding president of the Hong Kong College of Physicians (HKCP). Professor Young, a council member of the HKCP, helped determine the standard of practice and provide accreditation for specialists in medicine, following the example of the Royal Colleges of Physicians in the UK. Soon colleges were established for different specialties. The Academy of Medicine was founded in 1993 to coordinate the activities of all the colleges in Hong Kong and to establish guidelines to ensure integrity and ethical behaviour among doctors.[18] As a result, Hong Kong would become independent of the Royal Colleges in the UK after the handover in 1997. For his contributions, Professor Todd was knighted.[19]

Professor Rosie Young would distinguish herself for her service in other settings and receive multiple honours. Throughout her working life, however, she remained dedicated to the Department of Medicine and continued to keep an eye on it and to help her juniors. She became a matriarch and is greatly respected by everyone.

A Taste of Administration

As Hong Kong evolved into a regional manufacturing hub, its economy kept pace, averaging 8.1 per cent growth during the decade from 1973 to 1982. The boom of the 1970s enabled the reform-minded Governor Murray MacLehose to deviate from Hong Kong's traditional economic policy and spend generously on public projects. In 1972, he announced the ambitious Ten-year Housing Programme to resettle 1.9 million people. Medical and health services and educational amenities were greatly expanded and extra funding was allotted to social welfare.[20] Long-

---

18. Hong Kong Academy of Medicine, *In Pursuit of Excellence: The First 10 Years, 1993–2003* (Hong Kong: Hong Kong Academy of Medicine, 2003), 52–54.
19. 'A Knight Hospitaler', *South China Morning Post*, 2 July 1995.
20. *Hong Kong Annual Report*, 1968, 10.

term plans were developed for each of these services.[21] It was during this period that the citizens started to call themselves 'Hongkongers'.

As the expiry of the lease of the New Territories loomed, Sino-British negotiations began in 1982. Although there was a setback in the economy as talks stalled, it bounced back with the signing of the Sino-British Joint Declaration in 1984, when people's confidence in the future of Hong Kong returned. As China opened up and began industrialization, most factories in Hong Kong moved to southern China to take advantage of the cheap labour. Hong Kong's solid industrial base, excellent trade network, modern banking, insurance, and other business services, vibrant domestically driven economy, and an increasingly educated workforce all helped transform it into a leading international financial centre.[22]

It was against this socio-economic and political backdrop that Professor Young would realize her full potential.

Professor Young had had her first taste of university administration before Old Mac left. While she was waiting for her promotion to professorship to be approved by the university authorities, she received an invitation from Professor Rayson Huang, the first Chinese vice-chancellor of HKU, to join the Development and General Purpose Committee (D&GPC). The D&GPC later became the General Purpose Committee (GPC). A senior management team was established following the recommendations of the 'Fit for Purpose' Report published in 2003.[23] It met regularly to discuss important university issues and advise the vice-chancellor, but it did not replace the GPC, which reported to the Senate and the HKU Council. When Professor McFadzean learned of her appointment to the D&GPC, he objected, worried it would divert her attention from research. Professor Young, however, felt that if the university had a need for her, she would do her best to help.

---

21. Hong Kong Legislative Council Debates Official Report. In the Session of the Legislative Council of Hong Kong Which Opened 17 October 1973 in the Twenty-Second Year of the Reign of her Majesty Queen Elizabeth II.
22. Tsang, *A Modern History of Hong Kong*, 174.
23. 'Fit for Purpose', Report of a Review Panel chaired by Professor John Niland of University of New South Wales, submitted to HKU R10, in February 2003, accessed 15 August 2023, https://www.hku.hk/press/news_detail_5985.html.

The retirement and subsequent death of Professor McFadzean brought changes to Professor Young's work life. She felt Old Mac's loss deeply. As in the past, she coped with the loss by working harder, keeping herself fully occupied with no time to dwell on the pain. During the following decades, she would gradually shift her focus from research, which she had enjoyed so much, to administration and public service.

Immersion in University Administration and Public Service

In those days at HKU, deans were nominated by members of the respective faculty. In 1978, Professor Young and some of her colleagues nominated Dr Arnold Hsieh, professor of physiology, to be the next dean when the position became vacant, not realizing the significance of having someone in basic science in this position. Shortly after, Professor Young was asked by Professor Hsieh to become the sub-dean to assist in all clinical matters. Professor Hsieh, a graduate of the medical school at St. John's University, Shanghai, was not eligible to practise medicine in Hong Kong according to the Medical Registration Ordinance, which permitted only local graduates to practise in the city. That meant Professor Hsieh was not familiar with matters related to local practice of medicine. Professor Young, feeling compelled to help Professor Hsieh because she nominated him, served as sub-dean of the Faculty of Medicine from 1978 to 1983. She did so well in the position that when Professor Hsieh's term ended, she was asked to take up the deanship. In 1985, she resigned as dean of the Faculty of Medicine when she was appointed by Professor Rayson Huang to be pro-vice-chancellor, a position she held until 1993.

As sub-dean of the faculty, Professor Young represented HKU at the Hong Kong Medical Council. She became deeply immersed in the council's affairs as chairman of the Licentiate Committee from 1986 to 1988 and as chairman of the Medical Council from 1988 to 1996.

Professor Young's administrative duties in the university and in public services were so numerous in the 1980s and 1990s that she was not able to spend much time at Queen Mary Hospital. She spent less and less time on research and more and more time in meetings, just as Old Mac had predicted. She retained all her teaching sessions but gave up clinical work and research, leaving them in the hands of her competent junior colleagues. During this period, she did something that was previously unheard of. She requested that the university reduce her salary by 50 per cent since she was only performing half of her duties—teaching and administration. The university recognized her generosity and provided accommodation for her. Her decision, however, set an unpopular precedent at the university since it became the rule for staff in similar situations. Appointments by the government for this type of service are usually honorary yet essential to the prestige and community standing of the university; many felt retaining their full university salaries would be fair as well as necessary for supporting a family.

Professor Young's contributions to public service in medicine were innumerable. In her various roles, she participated in the planning and implementation of reforms in the 1980s and 1990s that shaped the medical and health services of Hong Kong today. Her public service extended well beyond the medical field too. When her term as pro-vice-chancellor of HKU ended, she was invited by the government to chair the Education Commission (EC), a body established in 1984 on the recommendation of the Organisation for Economic Co-operation and Development (OECD) panel to advise the government on the overall development of education in the light of the community's needs. Professor Young served as chairman of the EC from 1993 to 1998 and was responsible for the publication of *Education Commission Reports* (ECR) *6*[24] and *7*.[25] Her contributions to HKU in administration, and to public service in medical and educational arenas, will be discussed in detail in Chapters 4, 5, and 6.

---

24. *Education Commission Report No. 6*, Education Bureau, Hong Kong Government, accessed 16 February 2023, https://www.e-c.edu.hk/doc/en/publications_and_related_documents/education_reports/ecr6_e.pdf.
25. *Education Commission Report No. 7*, Quality of Education, September 1997, accessed 16 February 2023, https://www.e-c.edu.hk/doc/en/publications_and_related_documents/education_reports/ecr7_e_2.pdf.

Approaching the Handover

Emigrating to other parts of the world is one way Hong Kong citizens respond to political challenges and upheavals. The first post-war wave of emigration occurred after the communist-inspired riots in 1967, the second wave after the signing of the Sino-British Joint Statement in 1984, and the third wave after the Tiananmen Square incident in 1989. The fourth wave, which began after the protests in June 2019, continues to the present day. Many people love their lives in Hong Kong, a fast-paced, exciting, and prosperous city, whose citizens have enjoyed personal and press freedom in a place that they have participated in building over the years. Many who left after the 1989 Tiananmen Square incident returned to Hong Kong in the 1990s, when the situation in China appeared to have stabilized. After their father passed away in 1985, Professor Young's siblings and their families followed the general trend, migrating to the UK, Australia, and the US. Professor Young thought well of the medical system in Australia, and she made a successful application to join members of her family there. By the time she had packed up her belongings and was ready to leave, nearly all of her family in Australia had returned to Hong Kong. At the time of the handover on 1 July 1997, everything appeared to be going well. In her mid-sixties, still active and full of energy, engaging in meaningful public service, Professor Young was not quite ready for a quiet life of retirement in Australia, and she unpacked her luggage with relief.

A Working Retirement

Since the 1980s, Professor Young had watched with eagerness the progressive industrialization, growth in economy, and increasing openness of China. She believed a strong China would be good for Chinese people in China and those abroad. She could not help but feel excited and proud when Hong Kong was finally returned to China in 1997, as did many others in Hong Kong then. But soon after the establishment of the Hong Kong SAR, the city was hit by a series of disasters. The Asian financial crisis, starting in Thailand in July 1997, wreaked havoc in Asian markets. Although Hong Kong came out relatively unscathed, its economy took time to recover. Towards the latter part of that year, avian influenza

(H5N1) hit Hong Kong, and a major epidemic was averted by culling over a million chickens.[26]

Many people did not realize that Professor Young had officially retired from HKU in 1999, because she continued with her usual activities. Age had not slowed her down. Every day, she climbed the four flights of stairs to her office rather than taking an elevator. She responded favourably to the university's requests for assistance, agreeing to chair the Board of Hong Kong University Foundation for Educational Development and Research, and becoming a member of the University Council. Although she had stepped down from chairmanship of the Medical Council and the EC by then, she was invited to chair ad hoc committees on medical and educational issues whenever her wisdom and experience were required. In 2003, a mysterious pneumonia known as severe acute respiratory syndrome (SARS) began in South China and spread to Hong Kong, affecting thousands and killing 299 people, including a number of doctors and nurses.[27] In the aftermath, Professor Young was asked to be one of the two Hong Kong representatives on the SARS Expert Committee. This was followed by an invitation to join the Monitoring Committee to ensure the implementation of the SARS Expert Committee's recommendations. In education, she continued to actively help post-secondary institutions such as the Caritas Institute of Higher Education and the Chinese Foundation Secondary School as well as chairing scholarship committees for various agencies.

After her official retirement, Professor Rosie Young was asked whether she regretted her decision to switch from an exciting research career to administration and public service. Her immediate reaction was that she found administration and public service meaningful, satisfying, and beneficial to the community; moreover, in the 1970s, the university needed her help. Later, after giving the question more serious thought, she admitted that in the 1970s, she had felt that her own research was not remarkable because her studies were limited to using physiological and

---

26. Moira M. W. Chan-Yeung, *A Medical History of Hong Kong, 1942–2015* (Hong Kong: Chinese University of Hong Kong Press, 2019), 148–49.
27. Chan-Yeung, *A Medical History of Hong Kong*, 154–56.

biological methods which, while adequate for clinical research, were inadequate for basic science research. Research grants were hard to obtain and research facilities limited at that time. The laboratories in the university lacked up-to-date equipment for basic science research, and services for the equipment were problematic.

From this distance, it is clear that Professor Young had modestly underestimated the impact of her own research. Even though it was limited to using physiological and biological methods, she conducted very meaningful clinical research. She described two new syndromes that led to the treatment and prevention of these conditions: hypoglycaemia in patients with hepatocellular carcinoma and periodic paralysis in patients with thyrotoxicosis. Her research also opened up new avenues to further studies that would increase our understanding of carbohydrate metabolism. In 1989, she was awarded the Daiichi-Mallinckrodt Prize at the 4th Asia and Oceania Thyroid Association meeting in Seoul, Korea, for her research in thyroid diseases—a testimony to her originality and skills in research.

Figure 3.5: Professor Young awarded the Daiichi-Malinckrodt Prize at the Fourth Asia and Oceania Thyroid Association in Korea, 1989.

Perhaps there were other reasons for her to shift the direction of her career. She must have done a great deal of soul searching after the departure of Old Mac, as would anyone in her position, and came to the conclusion that her main goal in life is to serve the community and there are many ways of doing so. Once she found that the impact of administration and public service could be far reaching, she decided to continue. For whatever her reason, we can be thankful to Professor Young for her shift in focus to administration and public service, where she devoted herself to reforming medical and educational services and to enriching the community.

Professor Young's ninetieth birthday in 2020 was celebrated by several happy events at the university with colleagues she regarded as family. Many interviews with her were aired on television. Colleagues and friends contributed over HK$1 million to establish the Rosie Young 90 Medal for Outstanding Young Woman Scholar,[28] honouring Professor Young's immense achievements and contributions. The medal recognizes talented young academics and encourages them to follow in her illustrious footsteps. Each year, there will be one awardee from the Faculty of Medicine and one from non-medical disciplines. In addition, the HKU Foundation, of which she has been the chairman of the board since 2012, also established the HKU iGift-Rosie Young Scarf program.[29] There were altogether 7,004 iGifters who donated a total of HK$9.24 million. Each donor received the Rosie Young Signature Scarf. The funds raised benefitted ten faculties, the First-in-the-Family Education Fund, Scholarship Funds, and the President's Development Fund.

At the time of writing, Professor Young's life is less hectic. She continues to teach medical students and is responsible for two outpatient clinics each week at Queen Mary Hospital and two clinics at the Hong Kong Sanatorium and Hospitals, leaving Fridays for meetings. She reviews medical journals, and webinars put on by the various Royal Colleges in

---

28. 'Rosie Young 90 Medal for Outstanding Young Woman Scholar', accessed 6 August 2023, https://www.giving.hku.hk/rosie-young-90-medal-for-outstanding-young-woman-scholar/.
29. HKU iGift – Rosie Young Scarf, accessed 6 August 2023, https://igift.hku.hk/.

the UK, believing strongly in keeping one's medical knowledge up to date. For the first time in her life, she also indulges herself in watching DVDs on stories based on historical events in China.

Few people know that she maintains a collection of over one hundred dolls in her home. Whenever she travels, she makes it a habit to buy a doll, since dolls reflect so colourfully the culture and costumes of the location. The dolls she likes best are several she bought in Russia, having read the great Russian novels such as *War and Peace* and *Anna Karenina* in translation. In her love of dolls, she maintains a connection with her inner youthfulness.

In her younger days, Professor Young travelled extensively, visiting Europe, USA, Australia, and New Zealand during her postgraduate years, and later attending regional and international conferences to present her research findings or to give lectures. After her retirement, she travels less, but on weekends, she still likes to visit different areas around Hong Kong on public transport. She believes that academics should not live in an ivory tower but should know what is going on in their communities.

She remains active and energetic, talking as rapidly as ever and exhibiting an excellent memory that would make anyone envious. Her former students were often surprised when she called them by their first name and recalled when and where she first met them. When asked the keys to good health and longevity, she identified good genes, no drinking or smoking, a weight that is appropriate to one's height, regular exercise, and being honest with oneself and those around.

Professor Young has many loyalties and devotion in her life in addition to her own family: the Department of Medicine, the Faculty of Medicine, HKU, and the communities in Hong Kong and China. She has contributed enormously to the university and the larger community in Hong Kong. She appreciates the many opportunities to fulfil her potential as a scholar, a researcher, a physician, an educationalist, and an administrator. She feels deeply about the profound schism that has occurred in the community, among friends, and even within families in recent years. But she remains an eternal optimist, believing in a better tomorrow and looking forward to a bright future in Hong Kong.

Part 2

4

Blazing a Trail

University Administrator

The Development and General Purpose Committee, 1974

Rosie Young's first encounter with administration was a strange experience. In 1974, she was asked by HKU Vice-Chancellor Rayson Huang to join D&GPC. D&GPC was a joint committee of the council and senate to consider important university issues for recommendations to the parent bodies. The committee was made up of the most senior staff at the university; all were in the professorial rank, and some were deans. When Rosie walked into the meeting room for the first time, she saw mostly white men in their fifties and sixties. There was only one other woman, also white. Rosie was still waiting for the university to approve her promotion to professor, but the vice-chancellor believed that it would be beneficial to have more women and junior faculty members represented on the D&GPC.

Professor Huang opened the meeting by introducing Rosie. Immediately many hands were raised. A professor of philosophy asked why the committee had a new member who was not yet a professor. The discussion continued with Rosie present. She did not know how to excuse herself from the meeting, and she was not asked to leave. Professor Huang handled the situation well despite opposition. He referred Rosie's appointment to the University Senate even though senate approval was not required. In the end, Rosie was successfully appointed to the D&GPC. By then, her appointment as professor had been approved.

Professor Young had the greatest admiration for Professor Huang, who was the first Chinese vice-chancellor of HKU. A student at St. John's University in Shanghai when the Second World War began, Huang entered HKU in 1938. His education was further interrupted in 1941, when the Japanese occupied Hong Kong and he escaped to Free China. From China, in 1945, he followed the staff of the university's Chemistry Department to Oxford, where he completed his doctorate on a scholarship. After the war he joined the Chemistry Department at the University of Malaya and later became dean of the Faculty of Chemistry there. In 1969, he was appointed vice-chancellor of Nanyang University in Singapore, and in 1972, vice-chancellor of HKU.

Professor Huang became HKU's vice-chancellor at a time when colonialism prevailed in Hong Kong. Most senior staff at the university were white men. Accomplishing his work while managing the European staff was a major achievement indeed. Whenever there was a D&GPC meeting, for example, the deans might meet ahead of time to determine among themselves what they wanted the outcome to be in respect of various issues. That meant there could be not much to discuss at the meeting and all dean members voted the same way. Professor Huang knew what was going on but kept quiet. He would get what he wanted from the group by manoeuvring his way around after the meetings. As vice-chancellor, he was hard-working, resourceful, and often came up with great solutions to problems.

On the D&GPC, Professor Young listened, observed, and learned about the workings of HKU at the highest level. All this would be highly useful to her at a later date, when she became pro-vice-chancellor.

Sub-dean and Dean (1978–1985)

Professor Young became sub-dean of the Faculty of Medicine in 1978, at the request of the dean of medicine, Professor Arnold Hsieh. As sub-dean, she was in charge of medical students in their clinical years. She assisted Professor Hsieh during interviews with applicants for admission to the Faculty of Medicine. Interviews were also held with students who failed their undergraduate degree examinations, to find out what had happened and whether any help was necessary. During the Christmas season, Professor Young would invite students for a party at her home. Her father looked forward to the occasion every year. Her time as sub-dean placed her in close contact with students, and she felt that she did well with them. In addition, as noted, she became a member of the Hong Kong Medical Council to represent HKU.

In 1983, when Professor Hsieh retired, Professor Young became dean—the first female dean and the first HKU graduate to be appointed to the position. Gender bias in education and in the professions had persisted in Hong Kong. Universal education, which began in 1971 with primary education and included junior secondary education in 1978, would gradually right the gender bias in higher institutes of learning.[1] In 1961, males dominated the first-year entrants to HKU, and this was particularly so in the Faculty of Medicine. By 2020, of all the new entrants to HKU, 56 per cent were girls; in the Faculty of Medicine, the figure was 54 per cent.[2] In other parts of the Western world, gender changes had occurred in education too. In 2017, there were 30 per cent more girls than boys in universities in the UK, and girls did better than boys by about 8 percentage points at the General Certificate of Secondary Examination.[3]

Over the past few decades, the number of female faculty members at HKU, medical and non-medical, has also increased slowly. In 2021, males still dominated in the professorial rank, the ratio of male to female at 2.6:1; but in the lower academic levels, the ratio was reversed.[4] In 1957, Professor Daphne Chun was the first Chinese woman and a local graduate to be appointed to a professorial rank in the Department of Obstetrics and

---

1. Grace C. L. Mak, 'Women and Education', in *Women and Girls in Hong Kong: Current Situation and Future Challenges*, ed. Susanne Y. P. Choi and Fanny M. Cheung (Hong Kong: Hong Kong Institute of Asia-Pacific Studies, The Chinese University of Hong Kong, 2012), 24.
2. Information obtained from the Faculty of Medicine, HKU.
3. Gender and Educational Summary Grid for A Level Sociology. ReviseSociology, accessed 16 February 2023, https://revisesociology.com/2017/04/19/gender-and-education-summary-grid-for-a-level-sociology/.
4. *The University of Hong Kong Annual Report 2021*, accessed 2 February 2023, https://www4.hku.hk/pubunit/annualreport/ebook_AR2021/48-49/.

Figure 4.1: Professor Rosie Young, dean of the Faculty of Medicine, HKU, circa 1983.

Gynaecology. But Professor Young was the trailblazer in Hong Kong for women in academic administration.

As dean of the Faculty of Medicine, Professor Young enjoyed the support of the clinical departments. Professor David Todd of the Department of Medicine and Professor G. B. Ong of the Department of Surgery were two of Professor Young's most ardent supporters. With the backing of the heads of the two major departments, faculty meetings usually went smoothly.

The China Medical Board (CMB), formed in 1920 by the Rockefeller Foundation, focused on development of Western medical education in China. The board established Peking Union Medical College (PUMC). Hong Kong also benefited in receiving an endowment to establish three Rockefeller professorships which enabled HKU Faculty of Medicine to establish the clinical departments in the mid-1920s. After the establishment of the People's Republic of China in 1949, PUMC became nationalized, and the CMB had to withdraw from China. Between 1951 and 1973, the CMB brought more than 700 fellows from thirty leading institutions in Asia for advanced training in the US. Hong Kong also benefited from its fellowship programme. In addition to Professor Young, a number of HKU academic staff received the CMB Fellowship award. However, instead of returning to serve their own countries, many fellows ended up staying in the US. The CMB therefore discontinued the programme in the mid-1970s[5] and instituted another programme for the East Asian and Southeast Asian doctors to receive training in Hong Kong or Singapore, where medical development was considered advanced in East Asia, instead of going to the US. Through this scheme—the HKU/CMB Fellowship Programme, individuals, who received the fellowship award from Southeast Asia—had the opportunity to receive postgraduate studies in Hong Kong. When China opened up in the 1980s, academic exchanges between mainland China and Hong Kong were feasible, and a number of medical teachers from China were able to come to Hong Kong for further training.[6] Over the years, hundreds of doctors from the mainland have benefited from this programme. In 1991, the CMB programme was discontinued, but in Hong Kong, the programme remained through the generous donation from Dr Cheng Yu Tung.[7] Professor James Gibson (dean of the Faculty of Medicine, HKU, 1972–1978) was the chief architect in charge of this programme in Hong Kong until his retirement in 1983. Professor Young, as sub-dean and then dean, was responsible for the programme of placing candidates from China and Southeast Asia in the various departments in Faculty of Medicine. She was also a member of the selection committee to choose the best candidate from HKU for the CMB award to be trained at the US. In the 1980s, nurses were trained by major hospitals, as Hong Kong did not have a nursing school. When the CMB wanted to help China to train nurses, it approached the Hong Kong

---

5. Frank Ching, *130 years of Medicine in Hong Kong: From the College of Medicine for Chinese to Li Ka Shing Faculty of Medicine* (Singapore: Springer Nature, 2018), 326–38.
6. Citation: James Blackburn Gibson, Doctor of Science, *honoris causa*, 118th Congregation, 1983, The Hong Kong University.
7. Ching, *130 Years of Medicine in Hong Kong*, 346.

Medical and Health Department and obtained permission for candidates from China to be trained at Queen Mary Hospital. HKU was the conduit for this programme and Professor Young, as dean, helped to make this possible.[8]

Professor Young was dissatisfied with the medical curriculum at the time she became dean because it was far too full and included too many examinations, putting great pressure on students. She hoped to change the pedagogy in the Faculty of Medicine, to make teaching more interactive and allow the students more opportunities to express their opinions. She also hoped to foster a closer working relationship with the government to improve medical and health services in Hong Kong. Recognizing the importance of primary care and the lack of trained primary care doctors in Hong Kong, the faculty had begun planning for a new department of general practice, but it was difficult to find the appropriate individuals to teach it.[9] Professor Young was dean for just over one year before she stepped down to become HKU's pro-vice-chancellor, so she had to leave these projects to her successors.

As sub-dean, Professor Young often helped Professor Gerald Choa, the founding dean of the newly established medical school at the Chinese University of Hong Kong (CUHK), to interview applicants for faculty positions and potential students at the Faculty of Medicine of CUHK. Medical enrolment tripled at HKU between the 1950s and the 1970s, but the number of doctors produced still could not meet the demand of a mushrooming post-war population. In 1953, there were 0.29 doctors/1,000 population in Hong Kong.[10] By 1967, the number had risen to around 0.57/1,000 population.[11] In 1974, the Legislative Council

---

8. Ching, *130 Years of Medicine in Hong Kong*, 351.
9. 'Professor Young Tse Tse, Rosie, Dean of Faculty of Medicine', *Caduceus* 15, no. 4 (1983): 137–38.
10. *Hong Kong Medical and Health Department Annual Reports 1953–1990*, and *Hong Kong Annual Digest of Statistics*, 1991–2012.
11. *Hong Kong Statistics 1947 to 1967*, Census and Statistics Department, Hong Kong, 1969, accessed 20 February 2023. https://www.statistics.gov.hk/pub/hist/1961_1970/B10100031967AN67E0100.pdf.

and the government approved a second medical school at CUHK.[12] Plans included an attached 1,400-bed teaching hospital, the Prince of Wales Hospital, with both teaching and service units.[13] Dr Choa's leadership in the planning of the teaching hospital and the curriculum, as well as in recruiting staff, contributed greatly to the success of the new faculty.[14] The faculties of medicine at the two universities cooperated well during that period.

Pro-Vice-Chancellor (1985–1993)

Professor Young broke more new ground when she was appointed in 1985 as the first Chinese woman to become a pro-vice-chancellor of HKU. Such a high-level position in the central administration at the university had hitherto been the purview of Europeans. There were two pro-vice-chancellors at the time: Professor Kenneth Leonard Young and Professor Brian Lofts. Professor Rosie Young was appointed when Professor Lofts retired. There was no one more suitable than Professor Rosie Young, who proved to be an excellent administrator as dean of the Faculty of Medicine. By appointing her to the position, Vice-Chancellor Huang also challenged HKU's conservative image.

The Sino-British negotiations that began in 1982 were difficult and prolonged, and Hong Kong citizens were not represented in the process even though it would determine their future. People became jittery when there was no upbeat news after British Prime Minister Margaret Thatcher's visit to Beijing in September 1982. The Hong Kong stock market gradually lost its value and the local currency depreciated. As the negotiations reached an impasse in August 1983, Hong Kong's financial market reacted with panic, and by late September 1983, the Hong Kong dollar had fallen to a low of HK$9.5 to the US dollar, in contrast to HK$5.9 the previous year. Shortly afterwards, with the help of the Bank of England, the British

---

12. Arthur E. Starling, *The Chance of a Lifetime: The Birth of a New Medical School in Hong Kong* (Hong Kong: Chinese University Press of Hong Kong, 1988), 33.
13. Starling, *The Chance of a Lifetime*, 14–15.
14. Y.L. Yu, 'Reminiscences of Three Former Teachers: Prof AJS McFadzean, Dr Stephen Chang, and Prof Gerald Choa', *Hong Kong Medical Journal* 15, no. 4 (2009): 315–18.

and Hong Kong governments linked the local currency to the US dollar, to restore confidence.[15] The Sino-British Joint Declaration was finally signed in 1984.

As pro-vice-chancellor, Professor Young was responsible for human resources. The downturn of the economy had resulted in cuts to HKU funding, so the central administration had to cope with a smaller budget. Professor Huang as vice-chancellor froze all university positions, and there was no new hiring or promotion. He outsourced a number of services, such as janitorial and security, leading to considerable savings. And, instead of giving each department equal funding for research work, the university decided to offer grants on a competitive basis. This is a more effective way of encouraging research, and the university continues to support research on a competitive basis. Professor Huang also decentralized some administrative duties to the faculty level, including hiring of certain staff, reducing the administrative burden centrally. Although these methods were not new, Professor Young admired the vice-chancellor's resourcefulness. She began teaching young faculty members how to write research grant applications. Later, when she was heading the EC, she was in favour of school-based management, which aimed to decentralize administration to individual schools.

Vice-Chancellor Huang became a member of the Legislative Council[16] at the request of Governor Murray MacLehose, whom he had met during the war in China. He spent a great deal of time away from the university because of his civic duties, not only on the Legislative Council but also on government commissions, such as the Precious Blood Golden Jubilee Girls' School incident in 1978. Professor Huang took pains over the investigation to seek the truth, and he was away from the university for six weeks to find a satisfactory solution for the students.[17] Professor

---

15. Tsang, *A Modern History of Hong Kong*, 220–24.
16. Rayson Huang, *A Lifetime in Academia: An Autobiography* (Hong Kong: Hong Kong University Press, 2000), 147.
17. Students at that school had been boycotting classes and sitting quietly outside classrooms in protest over what they claimed was financial mismanagement at the school. The Education Department ordered the school closed without looking into the situation. Convinced that they were right, the students requested an audience with the

Huang was also recruited to the committee charged with drafting the Basic Law of Hong Kong, the mini constitution of HKSAR. During that time, he delegated a great deal of responsibility to his two pro-vice-chancellors. He asked Professor Rosie Young to interview all applicants for jobs below the level of professorship, while he continued to interview applicants for professorship. She gained considerable experience with interviews and in judging character. Professor Huang retired as vice-chancellor in 1986.

After his retirement, Professor Huang published an autobiography, entitled *A Lifetime in Academia*. In it, he revealed that Professor McFadzean was one of only two British professors who paid a visit to Huang's office to bid him welcome on his arrival at HKU. At HKU, Huang spent a great deal of time with students to understand how they felt and to hear about their frustrations. He was sympathetic with their dilemma; he wrote, 'They were youngsters without a country and their future was anything but certain or secure; for they were, in effect, citizens of neither Britain nor the People's Republic of China and where they called home was at best on "borrowed time in a borrowed place", to borrow a term from Han Suyin.'[18] Huang had not 'quelled a student demonstration during a royal visit to Hong Kong' in 1975, as was often said of him. Instead, he reasoned with student representatives by reminding them who the patron of HKU was and asking: 'How could we object to our patron coming to see us, especially on her first ever visit to Hong Kong? And how would Hong Kong University look to the people of Hong Kong if she did not call on us?' The students Queen Elizabeth II received in Hong Kong were the warmest and most enthusiastic ones she had seen in a long time.[19] This is just one example of Professor Huang's astuteness in dealing with sensitive political situations, which is clearly needed in a place such as Hong Kong.

    Catholic bishop, sitting outside the church in protest for three days before representatives of the bishop agreed to meet with them. The students returned to class, but the school was closed a second time on the order of the Education Department. Yee Wang Fung, 'An Analysis and Evaluation of the Precious Blood Golden Jubilee Girls' School Incident', *Ming Pao Monthly*, July 1978, 93–97.
18. Huang, *A Lifetime in Academia*, 142.
19. Huang, *A Lifetime in Academia*, 145.

Professor Huang also indicated in his book how grateful he was for all the assistance he had received from his pro-vice-chancellors over the years, particularly those from the Department of Medicine. He wrote, 'David [Todd] and Rosie, both medical graduates and distinguished academicians, were pillars of strength that the university was fortunate to have. They rendered sterling service not only to their alma mater, but also to the community in the field of health and medicine, and carried on this work beyond retirement.'[20]

Professor Wang Gungwu, a celebrated Indonesian-born historian, sinologist, and writer, succeeded Huang as vice-chancellor. As a historian of China and Southeast Asia, Professor Wang has studied and written about the history of China and Southeast Asia as well as the Chinese diaspora. He read history at the University of Malaya, where he received his bachelor's and master's degrees. He obtained a PhD from the School of Oriental and African Studies, University of London, in 1957. On his return to Malaya, he was appointed first as assistant lecturer at the University of Malaya, which was in both Singapore and Kuala Lumpur then, and rose rapidly to professorship in 1963. In 1968, he became professor of Far Eastern history in the Research School of Pacific and Asian Studies at the Australian National University and headed the Research School from 1975 to 1980. As a student of the University of Malaya at a time when it was gaining independence from the British, he was swept up in the political tide and became a founding member and the first president of the University Socialist Club at the University of Malaya. Later, as an academic staff member of the university, he became a founder of the Malaysian political party Gerakan though he was not directly involved in the party's activities.[21]

Professor Wang was invited to be vice-chancellor of HKU during the crucial transitional period before establishment of HKSAR in 1997. As a historian of China and Chinese overseas, he was deeply interested in the

---

20. Huang, *A Lifetime in Academia*, 135.
21. Lee Guan-kin, 'Wang Gungwu: An Oral History', in *Power and Identity in the Chinese World Order Festschrift in Honour of Professor Wang Gungwu*, ed. Billy So, John Fitzgerald, Jian Li Huang, and James K. Chin (Hong Kong: Hong Kong University Press, 2003), 375–405.

establishment of HKSAR, as it was a significant event in modern history, the history of China, and colonial history. He thought working in Hong Kong would facilitate his research on China, and he liked the unique cultural character of Hong Kong.

When Professor Wang became vice-chancellor in 1986, he was dismayed to find the poor Chinese and English standard among HKU students, which hindered their ability to learn, at variance with the students of the 1950s and 1960s. This poor standard of languages arose as a result of several significant sociopolitical changes in Hong Kong after that period. Waves of emigration from Hong Kong in the 1980s after the signing of the Joint Sino-British Agreement resulted in loss of middle and upper classes and many outstanding students from the city. The government's nine-year compulsory free education led to a sharp rise in the school population and candidates for higher education. The shortage of good teachers in schools, especially in the area of language learning, resulted in a decline of the standard. To deal with this problem, Professor Wang initially advocated a change of the three-year tertiary education system at HKU to a four-year one, hoping to improve the students' language skills during that year, but the proposal was met with resistance from secondary schools, and the four-year plan failed to materialize.[22] Nevertheless, he worked hard to improve the quality of research in natural and social sciences and to improve the interaction between scholars of HKU and those from the universities in China. He strengthened the ties between HKU alumni and the university and established a fund to support research in the Hong Kong University Foundation for Educational Development and Research. By 1997, HKU was ranked fourth among universities in Asia by *Asiaweek* magazine.[23]

Like Professor Huang, Professor Wang was appointed to the Executive Council and was chairman of both the Advisory Council on the Environment and the Council for Performing Arts. Additionally, being a leading scholar and historian, he was invited to address conferences and to attend meetings in different parts of the world. He depended on his

---

22. Lee, 'Wang Gungwu', 397–98.
23. Lee, 'Wang Gungwu', 398.

pro-vice-chancellors to hold the fort while he was away from his office. In 1988, Professor Cheung Yau Kai was appointed pro-vice chancellor at the retirement of Professor Kenneth Young, Professor A. J. Ellis was appointed as the third, and Professor Young became the senior pro-vice-chancellor. In 1991, Professor Ian Davis replaced Professor Ellis.

As pro-vice-chancellor, Professor Young served on many committees, including the Academic Development Committee, Committees Review Committee, Emeritus Professors Committee, Finance Committee, and General Purposes Committee. She also chaired committees concerning students such as the Committee on Students Affairs, the Board of Academic Awards, committees on staff matters such as Conditions of Service Committee, Committee on Personnel Matters, and Committee on Study Leave, and the Library Committee. She was a member of the University Court. One can appreciate the range of important services she provided, not only in the overall planning, development, and finance in the university but also in the well-being of the staff and students.[24]

In 1989, Professor Rosie Young encountered a crisis at HKU as a result of the Tiananmen Square incident. She had to handle the situation by herself at first, as Professor Wang was away from Hong Kong at the time. Even before 4 June, there were massive protests in Hong Kong in support of the Beijing students. On 27 May, over 300,000 people had gathered at Happy Valley Racecourse for an event called the Concert for Democracy in China. The following day, a procession of 1.5 million people, one-fourth of Hong Kong's population, led by Martin Lee, Szeto Wah, and others paraded through Hong Kong Island.[25] Following 4 June, there were even more protests and demonstrations. The end of May and beginning of June is the usual time for university examinations at HKU. Wishing to take part in the demonstrations, student representatives requested that Professor Young postpone the examinations. It was a decision not to be made readily. Fortunately for her, Professor Wang was returning home that evening. Professor Wang, who met with the students

---

24. Information obtained from Mrs Veronica Ho, head of General Records office, HKU.
25. Chris Yeung, 'Another Vast Crowd Joins World-Wide Show of Solidarity', *South China Morning Post*, 29 May 1989.

in the University Lodge that night, agreed to postpone the examinations. The students had also requested Professor Young take part in the demonstrations. She declined the invitation. As a pro-vice-chancellor, she felt her presence might be construed as representing the position of the university.

The Tiananmen Square protests led to fears in Hong Kong that China would renege on its commitment of 'one country, two systems' following the impending establishment of HKSAR in 1997. For many, the Tiananmen Square incident served as a turning point, the moment when they lost trust in the Beijing government. This event, coupled with general uncertainty about the status of Hong Kong after the transfer of sovereignty, led to further exodus of people from Hong Kong, including employees of HKU, to Western countries such as Canada and Australia.[26] The requests from some senior staff for a no-pay leave of three to five years to enable them to obtain residency status in their adoptive country were problematic for the university. It meant keeping the positions open and hiring only hard-to-find temporary replacements in the interim. In addition, there was no guarantee that those granted a no-pay-leave would return afterwards. The university decided to offer the leave to a small number of deserving staff, and Professor Young was given the unenviable task of making the selection from a large number of applicants. She went through stacks of curricula and interviewed each applicant carefully. Fortunately, the few staff members to whom she granted the no-pay leave all returned.

In 1993, after her term as senior pro-vice-chancellor ended, Professor Young was appointed chair of the Hong Kong Education Commission and chair of the Language Fund Advisory Committee, keeping her very busy. When Professor Wang retired from HKU in 1996, she was asked to serve as interim vice-chancellor, which might have led to her appointment as vice-chancellor. She declined, saying that she had no such ambition. The Tiananmen Square incident might have alerted her to the likely possibility of more politically sensitive issues arising in the future with the impending handover. She believed that she did not have the exceptional political

---

26. Government Information Report, 'Hong Kong Population: Characteristics and Trends', accessed 16 February 2023, https://www.info.gov.hk/info/population/eng/pdf/report_eng.pdf.

acumen and skills as did Professor Huang and Professor Wang. However, she agreed to serve as acting pro-vice-chancellor for one year, from 1996 to 1997, when she was in charge of staff and student affairs and resource allocation, and as acting dean of students from 1997 to 1999. As acting dean of students, she became a member of the Committees of Catering, Halls and Personal Development and Counselling, and a member of the Senate. She conducted a review of student services and the title of Dean of Students was changed to Dean of Student Affairs in 1999, to reflect the true nature of the job.

A Member of The University Council (2015–2020)

Since 2003, there had been a number of political disturbances with increasing frequency in Hong Kong. More recently, there were two major protests: the Umbrella Movement, which started on 1 October 2014, the Occupy Central Movement, a civil disobedience movement initiated about a week earlier, and the massive protests against the Extradition Bill in 2019. It is inevitable that some students and staff of institutes of higher learning were actively involved. HKU was not spared. It underwent a most tumultuous and painful period during which the University Council made several decisions to quell the unrests and to restore a peaceful and learning environment in the campus. These included the resolution not to appoint Professor Johannes Chan Man-mun, dean of the Faculty of Law, as pro-vice-chancellor even though he was unanimously recommended by the Senate Search Committee in 2015, and not to renew his contract in 2020, because he failed to prevent Professor Benny Tai in his department from initiating the Occupy Central Movement;[27] the dismissal of Professor Benny Tai in the same year because he was one of the three founders of the above movement;[28] and the closure of the HKU Student

---

27. Lilian Cheng, 'Outspoken Hong Kong Law Professor Johannes Chan "Has Left Post at End of HKU Contract"', *South China Morning Post*, 9 July 2021.
28. 'Benny Tai: Hong Kong University Fires Professor Who Led Protests', *BBC News*, 28 July 2020, accessed 22 February 2023, https://www.bbc.com/news/world-asia-china-53567333. The other two founders of the Occupy Central Movement were the Reverend Chu Yiu-ming of Chai Wan Baptist Church and Chan Kin-man, former associate professor of sociology at the Chinese University of Hong Kong.

Union in 2021 because it injudiciously passed a motion in memoriam to a deceased assailant on 7 July 2021.[29]

During the period from 2003 to 2015, the university's governing structure and practice changed. After the implementation of the recommendations of Niland's 'Fit for Purpose' report which was published in 2003,[30] the composition of the HKU Council altered. Of the twenty-four members in the council, there were fifteen lay members and nine university staff and students; thus, the university staff and students were outnumbered by lay members. The chancellor of HKU, as in all publicly funded universities in Hong Kong, is the chief executive of Hong Kong Special Administrative Region, just as the governor was during the British colonial administration. In 2015, the University Grants Council introduced new rules and practices aiming at improving the accountability of universities in Hong Kong and their governing bodies.[31] The roles of governance and management of the university were more clearly defined. The council was given more power and responsibilities. The changes in the composition of

---

29. 'HKU Responds to the Recent HKUSU Council', 8 July 2021, Statement of the University of Hong Kong, accessed 28 February 2023, https://www.hku.hk/press/news_detail_22996.html; 'Statement by the University of Hong Kong Concerning the HKUSU Council Incident', 13 July 2021, accessed 22 February 2023, https://hku.hk/press/news_detail_23017.html#:~:text=%22The%20University%20of%20Hong%20Kong,of%20the%20entire%20HKU%20community; Tony Cheung and Lilian Cheng, 'Hong Kong University Cuts Ties with Student Union Hours after Carrie Lam Expresses Anger over Motion Backing Man Who Stabbed Police Officer', *South China Morning Post*, 13 July 2021, accessed 28 February 2023, https://www.scmp.com/news/hong-kong/politics/article/3140882/hong-kong-leader-carrie-lam-very-angry-and-urges-further; and 港大學生會撤回悼念議案　幹事會解散致歉　三聯會撤清關係, Redbrick Society PressCom, accessed 28 February 2023, https://www.facebook.com/305868249479813/posts/4166475363419063/?paipv=0&eav=AfZGTx2aBIc-IPJ1r1hnfOB0q_IC1IsYjLLW53CMtIHJt0ecpPWvaOviF0ap82Iss60&_rdr.
30. 'Fit for Purpose', Report of a Review Panel chaired by Professor John Niland of University of New South Wales, submitted to HKU, February 2003, accessed 15 August 2023, https://www.hku.hk/press/news_detail_5985.html.
31. Sir Edward Newby, 'Governance in UGC-Funded Higher Education Institutions in Hong Kong', Report of the University Grants Committee, 2015, accessed 20 August 2023, https://www.ugc.edu.hk/doc/eng/ugc/publication/report/report20160330/full.pdf.

the membership of the council and the governing structure and practice of the university resulted in the council and its chairman becoming more involved in and having a much tighter control of university affairs.

Professor Young was appointed to serve on the HKU Council in September 2015, and Professor Arthur Li was appointed in 2016 as council chairman by the HKU chancellor, the chief executive of Hong Kong. Both Professor Young and Professor Li had served together on the Medical Council and on committees of other boards, when they often had serious arguments. However, while serving on the University Council, there was little argument between them. Apart from sitting on the council, Professor Young was an influential member of other committees, including the Discrimination Complaints Committee, the Elections Complaint Committee, and the Staff Grievances Committee,[32] yet she was not included in the Selection Committee for the new vice-chancellor in 2018. In 2021, Professor Young stepped down as a member of the HKU Council when her term ended.

Chairman of the Board of Directors, HKU Foundation (2012–Present)

At the time of writing, Professor Young is still the chairman of the Board of Directors of The University of Hong Kong Foundation for Educational Development and Research (HKU Foundation), a position which she assumed in 2012. She will be stepping down from the Foundation chair in October 2023. The foundation was established in 1995 as a charitable organization to support the university's dream and advancement. It comprises individual and corporate benefactors who share the mission of the university. The foundation has supported a host of projects in various areas through its investment income, with the aim of benefiting local as well as global communities. Donations to the university can be designated for specific projects or units in accordance with the benefactors' wishes. Since its establishment, the foundation has brought in millions of dollars

---

32. Information obtained from Mr Henry Wai, secretary of the Faculty of Medicine (1982–1987), and assistant registrar (2000–2002) and later registrar of HKU (2002–2022).

of donations for campus development, endowed professorships, and scholarships and bursaries for student support, and support for research.[33] Professor Young often met with potential donors, explaining to them HKU's mission, the areas that require development and support, and she met with them after the donations had been made to express the university's gratitude and appreciation. Her standing in the university and in the community and her persuasiveness helped bring in substantial donations.

Her Contributions to HKU Administration

Professor Young was sub-dean and dean of the Faculty of Medicine from 1978 to 1985 and was at the core of decision-making processes in HKU administration as a pro-vice-chancellor from 1985 to 1993, and acting pro-vice-chancellor, and later, dean of students from 1996 to 1999. This period coincided with the occurrence of historic events that caused considerable sociopolitical upheaval in Hong Kong. Despite the disturbances, HKU greatly expanded between 1978 and 1999, as a result of increasing demand for higher education and government support. In 1978, there were only three universities in Hong Kong, and by 1999, a total of eight universities were supported by the University Grants Committee.[34] In HKU, the undergraduate and postgraduate student enrolment increased from around 5,166 in 1978 to 14,570 in 1999.[35] Six new faculties and schools were created during this period: Dentistry (1982), the School of Architecture, the School of Education (now the Faculty of Architecture and the Faculty of Education) (1984), the Faculty of Law (1984), the School of Professional and Continuous Education (SPACE) (1992), and

---

33. 'The University of Hong Kong Foundation for Educational Development and Research', accessed 29 July 2023, https://www.giving.hku.hk/hku-foundation/about.
34. University Grants Committee, accessed 11 August 2023, https://www.ugc.edu.hk/eng/ugc/about/overview/history.html.
35. Student numbers were extracted from the *Vice-Chancellor's Reports* from 1978 to 1991 and from statistical booklets for 1992 and 1993. Those from 1994 were obtained from 'Introducing the University of Hong Kong' booklet and from 1995 to 1999, from *The Review*. All publications of HKU courtesy of Mrs Veronica Ho, head of the General Records Office, HKU.

the School of Business (now the Faculty of Business and Economics) (1995).[36] The university also underwent an extensive building program when thirty-four new buildings were erected to replace some of the old ones and to accommodate the six new faculties and schools with their students and staff, as well as new facilities such as the library and residences.[37]

The university at the time adopted a policy of a bottom-up approach in the planning process. Proposals, which were submitted by the faculties, were discussed by the Senior Management Committee which was chaired by the vice-chancellor. The decision-making process was, therefore, a collective one. The three pro-vice chancellors met almost every day to discuss the implementation of the decisions, problems arising from the implementation, and other matters. Professor Young modestly did not claim any specific contributions of her own. However, one can appreciate from the number of committees she chaired on staff and student affairs that she did much to improve the life and general well-being of the staff and students during this period. Her kindness, willingness to help, fairness, and honesty, improved the staff-student relationship in the university. Her role in the implementation of the initiative for faculty members to obtain internal university funding for research by competition and not by allocation and her innovation to teach junior academic staff to prepare better grant applications improved the competitiveness of HKU to obtain funds for research from external sources, thereby increasing the research capacities of the university and advancing the academic standing and reputation of the university. Even after her retirement, her work as chairman of the Board of the HKU Foundation brought in considerable donations for further development of the university in many areas.

Professor Young is an icon of the university. Her devotion, hard work, integrity, and fairmindedness won the respect and admiration from all students and staff in the university, especially those in the Faculty of Medicine.

---

36. Stacey Belcher Gould and Tina Yee-wang Pang, *HKU Memories from the Archives* (Hong Kong: HKU Museum and Art Gallery, 2013).
37. 'New Buildings Erected at HKU between 1980 and 2000', accessed 6 August 2023, https://www.estates.hku.hk/campus-information/hku-buildings-and-developments.

5

A True Holistic Approach

Public Service in Medicine

The Hong Kong Medical Council (1978–1996)

Professor Rosie Young became a member of the Hong Kong Medical Council when she was appointed sub-dean of HKU's Faculty of Medicine in 1978. This council was established in 1957, under the Medical Registration Ordinance Chapter 161, Laws of Hong Kong.[1] The council was founded to develop and maintain high standards in the medical profession, in order to protect patients and foster ethical conduct. It handles the registration of eligible medical practitioners, administers the Licensing Examination, issues a Code of Professional Conduct and Guidelines, and maps out a disciplinary mechanism to handle complaints lodged by members of the public and to exercise disciplinary action to the medical practitioners involved.

Professor Young's major contributions to the Hong Kong Medical Council began in 1986, when she was appointed simultaneously chairman of the council's Licentiate Committee and a member of the Working Party on Postgraduate Medical Education and Training. In 1988, when

---

1. 'Medical Registration: First Reading of the Bill to be Moved at the Meeting', *South China Morning Post*, 10 April 1957. Medical Registration Ordinance Cap 161 was enacted on 1/6/1957, accessed 4 March 2023, https://www.elegislation.gov.hk/hk/cap161!en?INDEX_CS=N&xpid=ID_1438402758342_001.

she became chairman of the Medical Council, she advocated critical reforms to meet the increasing demands on the council and to adapt to the changing political reality as the establishment of the HKSAR approached. The transformation of Hong Kong into a SAR of the People's Republic of China would have considerable implications for the medical system. To that point, Hong Kong doctors had been recognized by the General Medical Council of Britain, and doctors from Britain and other Commonwealth countries were allowed to practise in Hong Kong. As set out in the Sino-British Joint Declaration, Hong Kong would no longer be under British administration or part of the Commonwealth after 1997. Two issues arose from that: (1) the subsequent training and certifying of Hong Kong's specialists, which had been carried out by the Medical Royal Colleges in the UK;[2] and (2) the question of whether medical graduates from Britain and other Commonwealth countries would be required to take the licentiate examination for registration to practise in Hong Kong.

After the war, postgraduate training in Hong Kong was informal, medical graduates initially learning as apprentices of their seniors. After three to four years, they would travel to the UK for further professional training. Most of them returned with higher qualifications awarded by the Medical Royal Colleges, and some also obtained a university doctorate.[3] As early as 1968, the Medical Council had expressed interest in introducing specialist registration, but nothing much was done. The signing of the Sino-British Joint Declaration revived the issue. In 1986, the government established the Working Party on Postgraduate Medical Education and Training, chaired by Professor Keith E. Halnan, former director of the Department of Clinical Oncology at the Royal Postgraduate Medical School, London. Professor Young was invited to join the committee.

The Working Party consulted the public widely. In 1987, it issued a green paper that was discussed at public meetings. In the following year, a final report was submitted to the government. The Halnan Report's main

---

2. Hong Kong Academy of Medicine, *In Pursuit of Excellence: The First 10 years 1993–2003* (Hong Kong: Hong Kong Academy of Medicine Press, 2003), 11.
3. David Todd, 'Recent Developments in Medical Education in Hong Kong', in *Plague, SARS and the Story of Medicine in Hong Kong*, Hong Kong Museum of Medical Science Society (Hong Kong: Hong Kong University Press, 2006), 287–88.

recommendation was the establishment of an Academy of Medicine to supervise training, set postgraduate qualifications, and conduct examinations. The government appointed Professor David Todd as chairman of the academy's preparatory committee.[4] Following this, the Hong Kong College of Physicians and a number of other colleges for different specialties were formed. In 1993, the academy was established, with Professor Todd as the founding president.

The Halnan Report also recommended that the Hong Kong Medical Council be given the power to set up registration for specialists to protect patients from inadequately trained doctors.[5] Only those on the Specialist Register would be allowed to call themselves specialists, and others could be prosecuted for doing so. The report recommended that an education committee with representation from the two universities and different colleges should also be set up. The Medical Council would delegate power to the two universities and the academy to award undergraduate and postgraduate qualifications but remain responsible for the monitoring of curriculum content and standards. Two registers would be maintained: a register of doctors competent to practise and a specialist register. The government's Medical Registration (Amendment) Bill 1995 was enacted to make the Medical Council's new role official.[6] As chairman of the Hong Kong Medical Council, Professor Young was responsible for seeing that all the recommendations of the Halnan Report were carried out.

Professor Young also chaired the Medical Council's Licentiate Committee from 1986 to 1988. One of the major functions of the Medical Council was to administer the Licensing Examination. Hong Kong's Medical Registration Ordinance,[7] which became effective on

---

4. K. E. Halnan, 'Report of The Hong Kong Government Working Party on Postgraduate Medical Education and Training' (Hong Kong: Hong Kong Government Printer), October 1988; Frank Ching, *130 Years of Medicine in Hong Kong: From the College of Medicine for Chinese to Li Ka Shing Faculty of Medicine* (Singapore: Springer Nature, 2018), 361–62.
5. Ching, *130 Years of Medicine in Hong Kong*, 366.
6. Hong Kong Hansard, 28 July 1995.
7. Medical Registration Ordinance Cap 161 was enacted on 1/6/1957, accessed 4 March 2023, https://www.elegislation.gov.hk/hk/cap161!en?INDEX_CS=N&xpid=ID_1438402758342_001.

1 July 1957, had stipulated that only medical graduates from HKU and Commonwealth countries could have their names placed in the medical register after serving in a hospital as an intern for twelve months.

After the war, there was an acute shortage of registered doctors in Hong Kong. Among the immigrants and refugees arriving in great numbers were well-qualified doctors who were trained in Western medicine and had been practising in China. To assist these doctors to obtain registration, the government offered a series of examinations during the 1950s and 1960s. For example, the government invited the Society of Apothecaries of London to conduct examinations in Hong Kong in 1958, 1959, and 1960. Successful candidates were awarded the LMSSA, London—a recognized and registrable medical qualification for the General Medical Council.[8] There was also a 1965 examination organized by a panel of specialists who scrutinized the credentials of the 'unregistrable doctors' and conducted a short oral examination. Those who passed the examination would be allowed to work in charitable clinics, which were then registered with exemption from the Medical Clinic Ordinance 1963 (Cap 343).[9]

The shortage of doctors continued into the 1970s despite medical student enrolment at HKU tripling since the war. The supply of doctors simply could not keep up with the dramatic increase in population. In 1974, a Working Party on Unregistrable Doctors was formed by the government under the chairmanship of Sir Ronald Holmes. The working party recommended that non-Commonwealth-trained doctors who fulfilled certain conditions and passed a special examination be permitted to register in Hong Kong with no restrictions. These doctors must have gone through five years of full-time medical training, have permission to live and work in Hong Kong, and be of good character before they were allowed to sit for a three-part examination held under the auspices of the Medical Council. The examination consisted of a multiple-choice written paper designed to test for professional knowledge, a simple test of written English, and an oral

---

8. Hong Kong Government, *Report of the Working Party on Unregistrable Doctors*, Colonial Secretariat, Hong Kong, 11 April 1975, 2.
9. Hong Kong Government, *Report of the Working Party on Unregistrable Doctors*, Colonial Secretariat, Hong Kong 11 April 1975, Clinics, 2–3; 'Report of Advisory Committee on Clinics' (Hong Kong: Government Printers, 1966), 3–5.

examination to test the applicant's ability to apply professional knowledge to clinical problems. Except for the written English test, the examination could be taken in either English or Chinese.[10] Successful candidates would serve an externship, during which they worked in a hospital during the day but did not have to take calls, for eighteen months before registration. The pass rate of the licensing examination was persistently low, about 15 per cent over a period of five years.[11] A review was carried out by the Medical Council, but because the standard of the examinations was already lower than that of the examination for students in the local medical schools, the Medical Council decided against lowering the standard further.[12] As chairman of the Licentiate Committee, Professor Young was responsible for ensuring that the standard for the licensing examination was upheld.

As 1997 drew near, the issue of the licensing examination of British and Commonwealth medical graduates came to the forefront. These medical graduates had been exempted from Hong Kong's licentiate examination so far, but after the establishment of the HKSAR, this exemption would be no longer tenable. The Medical Registration (Amendment) 1995, which was enacted by the Legislative Council to come into effect on 1 September 1996, required that all medical graduates other than those from local universities pass the universal licensing examination before they could practise medicine in Hong Kong.[13] However, there was also the question of whether local residents already enrolled in previously recognized medical institutions in Britain and Commonwealth countries would be given a grace period of exemption from taking the universal licensing examination. It seemed that a number of legislators had children studying medicine in Britain and Commonwealth countries. After a great deal of debate, the Medical Registration (Transitional Provisions) Bill 1997 was

---

10. 'Unregistered Doctors May Gain Approval', *South China Morning Post*, 31 August 1975; 'Action Being Taken on Doctor Scheme', *South China Morning Post*, 25 October 1975.
11. 'Doctor Shock: Only 15% Pass', *South China Morning Post*, 26 March 1977.
12. 'Medical Men Probe Doctor Exam System', *South China Morning Post*, 14 January 1982.
13. Medical Registration (Amendment) No. 87 of 1995, accessed 16 February 2023, https://www.elegislation.gov.hk/hk/1995/87!en.

passed to grant exemption to these graduates, despite objections from the representative of the medical profession.[14]

Another important function of the Medical Council was to maintain high professional standards, including conducting disciplinary hearings in response to patient complaints. The number of patient complaints grew from 27 in 1978 to 170 in 1995, and the number of cases requiring formal disciplinary hearings from four to twenty-nine in corresponding years. These hearings could be delayed for up to two years, because each hearing required a quorum of five from among the existing fourteen council members.[15]

Professor Young had called for revamping the Medical Council several times since 1992.[16] The number of registered medical doctors in Hong Kong increased from 3,029 in 1978 to 7,779 in 1995. Professor Young proposed increasing the number of members on the Medical Council.[17] Up to then, the council members were appointed by the governor, and the council was answerable only to the government and not the medical profession. She suggested that the Medical Council have elected members and that the governor's right to veto membership be abolished. She was concerned about the council's credibility after 1997, if the authorities continued to have a final say on the membership. The future Medical Council, she proposed, should also continue to work within the Medical Registration Ordinance and be responsible for registering doctors. There was no official response to these proposals until 1994, when the Hong Kong Medical Association pressured the government to amend the Medical Registration Bill to revamp the Medical Council.[18]

---

14. Medical Registration Ordinance (Transition) 1 July 1997, Part V Section 35, accessed 16 February 2023, https://www.elegislation.gov.hk/hk/cap161!en@1997-07-01T00:00:00?pmc=0&SEARCH_WITHIN_CAP_TXT =assessor&xpid=ID_15 23342232172_003&m=0&pm=1.
15. Medical Registration Ordinance, Part II, The Medical Council of Hong Kong, 4(2) Historical Laws of Hong Kong online, accessed 16 February 2023, https://oelawhk.lib.hku.hk/items/show/2734.
16. 'Proposal for Overhaul of Doctors' Panel', *South China Morning Post*, 9 March 1992.
17. 'Medical Board Faces Big Test', *South China Morning Post*, 29 December 1994.
18. 'Doctors Call for Revamp of HK Medical Council', *South China Morning Post*, 24 January 1994.

After the Medical Registration (Amendment) Ordinance 1995 on licensing examinations for non-local graduates was enacted,[19] the Secretary for Health and Welfare brought forward a new bill to the Legislative Council that incorporated the changes requested by the Medical Council. These included enlarging the membership of the Medical Council; establishing three statutory committees: a Health Committee, an Education and Accreditation Committee, and an Ethics Committee; and granting the Medical Council the power to prohibit the disclosure of information relating to an inquiry by the council or a hearing by the Health Committee 'if it is in the interests of the complainant, defendant or witness'. The bill was extensively debated, and in the end, the government agreed to increase the membership of the Medical Council from fourteen to twenty-four: twelve elected members, and twelve appointed ones, including two lay members. The bill also stipulated that the Medical Council should appoint a Preliminary Investigation Committee (PIC) composed of six members, one of whom would be a lay member; and the quorum of each PIC meeting would be three, including the committee chairman or deputy chairman or both. The functions of the PIC were to conduct preliminary investigations into complaints touching on any matter that might be inquired into by the council or heard by the Health Committee, to give advice on the matter relating to any registered medical practitioner, and to make recommendations to the council about holding an inquiry.[20]

In July 1996, a new Medical Council was formed according to the Medical Registration (Amendment) (No. 2) 1995. Following its passage, Professor Young announced that the council should have new blood and that she would stand down.[21] Before she did so, she made sure that future

---

19. Medical Registration (Amendment) Ordinance 1995, accessed 16 February 2023, https://www.elegislation.gov.hk/hk/1995/87!en.
20. Medical Registration (Amendment) (No. 2) Ordinance 1995, accessed 16 February 2023, https://www.elegislation.gov.hk/hk/1995/10/27/supp3/1. A Preliminary Investigation Committee (PIC) was established in 1957, when the Medical Council was established. It consisted of three members. The PIC established under the Medical Registration (Amendment) (No. 2) Ordinance 1995 increased the membership to six, and a quorum three was required for a meeting.
21. 'Radical Surgery for Medical Body', *South China Morning Post*, 14 July 1996.

meetings of the Medical Council would be open to the public. During the decades that ensued, membership of the Medical Council continued to increase to twenty-eight including four lay members in 1996[22] and to thirty-two with eight lay members in 2018.[23] This enlarged the pool of assessors to sit on the PIC and the Inquiry Panel, enhancing the efficiency of complaint investigation and the disciplinary inquiry mechanism.

During Professor Young's tenure as chairman, the Medical Council changed from a conservative institution into a more democratic and open one. A new registry was established for specialists. In addition, from 1996 onwards, all non-local medical graduates, from either Commonwealth or non-Commonwealth countries, were required to take the licentiate examination before they could be registered for practice in Hong Kong.

Primary Health Care (1989–1991)

Professor Young had always been interested in family medicine because of her elder brother's experience as a general practitioner. She had observed that patients could be treated and regain health under the care of a good family doctor without incurring the cost of a specialist. General practitioners enjoyed the special relationships they developed over the years with their patients—at least, this was the way general practitioners practised primary care before the war. When she became dean of the HKU Faculty of Medicine, Professor Young wanted to introduce family medicine, training primary care doctors either in a new department or a division within the Department of Medicine. However, her term as dean was short, just over one year. In 1989, when she was invited to chair the Working Party on Primary Health Care (WPPHC) in Hong Kong, she agreed to serve without hesitation.

Medical care in Hong Kong is delivered through two systems: public sector and private sector. The private sector provides about 85 per cent of primary medical care, and the public outpatient services covering the

---

22. Cap 161, Medical Registration (Amendment) Ordinance 1996, accessed 16 February 2023, https://www.elegislation.gov.hk/hk/1996/7!en.
23. Cap 161, Medical Registration (Amendment) Ordinance 2018, accessed 16 February 2023, https://www.elegislation.gov.hk/hk/cap161.

remaining 15 per cent. Because of the population explosion in Hong Kong after the war and the shortage of doctors, general practitioners, both in the private sector and in the government system, were able to treat patients only for acute illnesses. They rarely found time for the essential work of prevention and health promotion. During the 1970s, chronic non-communicable diseases, which could have been prevented in their progress by good primary care, became major causes of morbidity and mortality. At the same time, Hong Kong's residents were ageing, meaning a higher incidence of chronic non-communicable diseases and a higher utilization of health care resources.[24] Many doctors did not have the proper training to perform primary care services, and there was no primary care network to speak of. There were also persistent complaints of inadequate medical care in the public sector in the outpatient clinics,[25] the School Medical Service, and other services.[26] A stronger primary care system was badly needed in Hong Kong.

In 1978, when the WHO promoted a primary health care approach as the key to achieving the goal of 'Health for All' by the year 2000, family medicine and general practice as a specialty remained underdeveloped and undervalued in Hong Kong. In 1989, the government established the WPPHC and invited Professor Young to chair it. The group consisted of seventeen other members, mostly drawn from various medical sectors: the two universities, the Hong Kong Medical Association, the Hong Kong Branch of the British Medical Association, the Hong Kong College of General Practitioners, the chairman of the School Medical Service Board, the director of Department of Health and his deputy, and a representative from each of the three government departments/branches: Hospital

---

24. World Bank, Population in Hong Kong, SAR, accessed 16 February 2023, https://data.worldbank.org/indicator/SP.POP.65UP.TO.ZS?end=2020&locations=HK&start=1960.
25. 'High Patient Quotas Affect Medical Care', *South China Morning Post*, 1 October 1990.
26. 'School Health Doctors May Work to Rule', *South China Morning Post*, 5 March 1989.

Services, Finance, and Health and Welfare.[27] The WPPHC was guided by the following terms of references, briefly:[28]

1) To review primary health care in Hong Kong with reference to the provision of general outpatient service, maternal and child health care including family planning, school medical service, health education, and immunization against major infectious diseases, and prevention and control of communicable and non-communicable disease;
2) To review the adequacy of arrangements for coordinating the various parts of the service;
3) To advise on the measures and changes needed to improve the delivery of primary health care to the public;
4) To suggest the arrangements needed to strengthen the coordination between general outpatient clinics and public hospitals including keeping patients out of hospitals and to encourage ambulatory care;
5) To consider whether general outpatient services and any other aspects of primary health care should be brought under the new organization, the Hospital Authority, which had the overall responsibility of all government and subvented hospitals (see below) in Hong Kong;
6) To examine the respective roles of public and private sectors and the educational bodies with the aim of achieving better coordination and cooperation among the sectors in the overall development of primary health care in Hong Kong; and
7) To assess the resource implications required for implementing the Working Party's recommendations.

The WPPHC proved a challenging group to work with because of the conflicting opinions among members. The administrative and political skill that Professor Young had honed as pro-vice-chancellor of HKU proved to be very helpful in getting a complex group of people to cooperate. Many members of the Working Party were also graduates of HKU who respected Professor Young because she had been their teacher or colleague. In addition, there was the problem of an ineffective secretary of the

---

27. 'Return to Basics in Primary Health Care', *South China Morning Post*, 6 August 1989.
28. *Report of the Working Party of Primary Health Care in Hong Kong*, 1990, 15–16.

A TRUE HOLISTIC APPROACH   103

Figure 5.1: The WPPHC Committee dinner, Professor Young (sitting, second from the right), Mrs Carrie Lam (sitting, first from the left), 1980.

Working Party, who tended not to issue the minutes of the previous meetings on time. This problem was solved when Professor Young insisted on a change of the secretary. Mrs Carrie Lam, principal assistant secretary, who was representative from the Health and Welfare Branch at the time,[29] responded promptly and ensured that meetings and record keeping proceeded smoothly. Mrs Lam's role with the WPPHC must have aroused her interest in primary care, as reforms hastened when she became the chief executive of Hong Kong from 2017 to 2022.

The terms of reference for the WPPHC were wide-ranging, involving a review of many different services in both the public and private sectors. While the Department of Health was providing free preventive services for all, like maternal and child health and immunization, in primary medical care, or first contact curative service, public general outpatient clinics were providing for 15 per cent of the medical consultations, as noted.

---

29. *Report of the Working Party of Primary Health Care in Hong Kong*, 15–16.

Since there was paucity of data on public outpatient services, the group commissioned a team of researchers from HKU to survey general outpatient clinics, the use of maternal and child health centres by mothers and children, and health care utilization by different populations. Professor Young's background as a researcher proved useful in guiding the research. The Department of Health also conducted a survey on the opinion of doctors working in general outpatient service and family health service. In addition, the WPPHC invited international experts to review various primary care services, public health nursing services, and training in family medicine. It also invited submissions from interested organizations and the public and gathered materials on primary care from other countries, provider associations, and professional bodies.[30] WPPHC members visited government clinics to assess the working environment and sent delegations to study primary health care services in Singapore[31] and to attend an international conference on health care systems in Taiwan.

A statistics group was assembled to analyse the data obtained. The WPPHC was also divided into groups that investigated specific areas of primary care such as health promotion, disease prevention, school health services, clinic services, and community services. Based on survey findings and submissions, each group, which had incorporated into its membership other professionals and experts in the field to obtain a wider representation of views, prepared recommendations in its respective area. A coordinating group was formed to finalize the report and its recommendations.[32]

In the report released on 28 December 1990, the WPPHC noted that it had had great difficulty conducting its review because of an unclear and outdated health care policy. There was an imbalance between hospital and primary health care services, the report stated; and a clear commitment to primary health care was badly needed. The report's 102 recommendations pertaining to preventive health care were wide-ranging, and

---

30. R. Gauld and D. Gould, *The Hong Kong Health Sector* (Hong Kong: Chinese University of Hong Kong Press, 2002), 75–77.
31. 'Health Trip to Singapore', *South China Morning Post*, 26 February 1990.
32. Gauld and Gould, *The Hong Kong Health Sector*, 77.

their implementations would require many new and costly initiatives,[33] including addressing the important role of occupational health services,[34] providing a health screening programme for students,[35] and improving rehabilitative services, especially in the delivery of home care. The report also emphasized the necessity of establishing a computer-based information system, vital for the continuity of care in general outpatient clinics under the Department of Health.[36]

General outpatient clinics lacked objectives, the WPPHC report continued, and a new set of guidelines would help the clinics to provide more effective, accessible, and quality services. The doctors in charge of the clinics needed proper training and a clear career path. Standards for private practitioners also needed upgrading, with an emphasis on their role in preventive medicine and health promotion. The report's recommendations were guidelines for the delivery of primary health care that would offer preventive, curative, and rehabilitative care in Hong Kong.[37]

The report did not receive much public attention. There were criticisms that the scope of the review of the WPPHC was too narrow, since it was limited to primary health care services in the public sector and neglected both the predominant private sector and practitioners of traditional Chinese medicine. Nevertheless, the recommendations pertaining to primary health care services were swiftly implemented by the Department of Health. By mid-1994, 98 of the 102 recommendations were officially carried out on the books, including the Student Health Service and screening services for well women and the elderly, and 68 per cent of the budget of the Department of Health had been channelled into primary health care services.[38] Some critics of the health care policy, however, found the exercise inconsequential, noting that the recommendations relating to primary medical care were barely implemented

---

33. *Working Party on Primary Health Care Report*, 1990, 8.
34. *Working Party on Primary Health Care Report*, 65–70.
35. *Working Party on Primary Health Care Report*, 87.
36. *Working Party on Primary Health Care Report*, 148.
37. *Working Party on Primary Health Care Report*, 143; 'Outpatient Services to Get Overhaul', *South China Morning Post*, 18 May 1991.
38. Gauld, and Gould, *The Hong Kong Health Sector*, 83.

in the private sector.[39] This criticism is perhaps unfair since the proposed reforms were costly[40] and it was not possible to carry them out all at once. Also, until more family physicians had been trained, reforms in primary care could not be carried out satisfactorily in the private sector.[41]

Primary care reform resumed in earnest after 2008, when a new Working Group on Primary Care was established, based on updated guidelines from the WHO[42] and the recommendations of the WPPHC. The following steps were taken in primary care reform:

(1) the development and implementation of reference frameworks for management of a number of common diseases such as hypertension and diabetes;[43]
(2) the establishment of a primary care directory, bringing various segments of primary care providers together to work as a multidisciplinary team;[44]
(3) the launching of community health centres offering one-stop, coordinated primary care services, including health-risk assessment and disease identification, disease prevention, health promotion and support for self-health awareness programmes;[45]
(4) the institution of electronic health-record sharing;

---

39. Gabriel M. Leung and John Bacon-Shone, *Hong Kong's Health System: Reflections, Perspectives and Visions* (Hong Kong: Hong Kong University Press, 2006), 145.
40. 'A Prescription for a Healthier Hong Kong', *South China Morning Post*, 25 April 1991.
41. 'Concern at Family Doctor Numbers', *South China Morning Post*, 13 May 1991.
42. *Primary Health Care. Now More than Ever*, The World Health Report 2008, accessed 16 February 2023, https://apps.who.int/iris/handle/10665/43949.
43. Hong Kong Reference Framework for Hypertension Care in the Primary Settings, 2016, accessed 16 February 2023, https://www.healthbureau.gov.hk/pho/files/e_hypertension_care_patient.pdf; Hong Kong Reference Framework for Diabetes Care in the Primary Settings, 2016, accessed 16 February 2023, https://www.healthbureau.gov.hk/pho/files/e_diabetes_care_patient.pdf.
44. *Primary Care Directory. Primary Care Initiatives*, accessed 19 September 2016, http://www.pco.gov.hk/english/initiatives/directory.html.
45. *Primary Care Initiatives*, accessed 15 February 2023, https://www.healthbureau.gov.hk/pho/main/primary_care_initiatives.html?lang=2.

(5) the initiation of an elderly health care voucher scheme[46] and a vaccination subsidy scheme to encourage the elderly to seek health care early and to take part in prevention services; and

(6) the promotion of training for family and primary care physicians.[47]

In 2022, the government announced a plan to establish a Primary Healthcare Authority to coordinate and govern primary health care services across the public and private sectors by 2024.[48] Professor Young was invited to open the Primary Healthcare Blueprint Symposium—Reform on the Road—on 15 January 2023.[49] A primary healthcare authority or commission[50] was what Professor Young had been proposing all along. Without such a body, she knew primary care reforms would be fragmentary in Hong Kong. Although Mrs Carrie Lam's mandate as chief executive ended in 2022, it is obvious that she was responsible for the above initiative. She did not consult Professor Young on this initiative, as she was fully cognizant of the problems associated with primary care and the recommendations of the WPPHC, having served as the representative from Health and Welfare Branch at that time. Professor Young's work with the WPPHC finally bore fruit decades later.

The Provisional Hospital Authority and the Hospital Authority (1988–1996)

Professor Young was appointed a member of the Provisional Hospital Authority Committee in 1988 and of the Hospital Authority Committee in 1990. Both committees were aimed at achieving a major overhaul of hospital services.

---

46. *Elderly Voucher Scheme, Primary Care Initiatives*, accessed 16 February 2023, https://www.hcv.gov.hk/en/hcvs/service_area.html.
47. Leung and Bacon-Shone, *Hong Kong's Health System*, 149.
48. 'Charting a Brighter Tomorrow for Hong Kong', The Chief Executive's 2022 Policy Address, HKSAR, 19 October 2022.
49. Primary Health Care Blueprint Symposium, accessed 22 February 2023, https://www.primaryhealthcare.gov.hk/tc/.
50. F. C. Pang and S. S. Lai, 'Establishment of the Primary Healthcare Commission', *Hong Kong Medical Journal* 29 (2023): 6–7.

Medical services expanded greatly between the 1970s and the 1990s with the growing affluence in Hong Kong. By 1984, the number of hospital beds had grown to 4.65/1,000 population from 2/1,000 in 1953, but hospitals remained as congested as before. Waiting times for non-urgent treatment could be longer than one year. Only critically ill patients were guaranteed prompt attention at government hospitals. Many government doctors clocked sixty- to eighty-hour work weeks, with little chance of promotion. They worked under poor conditions, often attending to patients in camp beds in corridors or on verandas. Many did not have an office or a desk, and there was no secretarial help. In the end, many doctors simply left the government Medical and Health Department for greener pastures. Patients complained about the situation as well. The response to calls for help was slow, the waiting time for bedpans was long, and bedside visits by doctors were infrequent. Amahs were rude, patients said, and nurses were indifferent. Hospital food was invariably poor and always cold by the time it arrived at bedside.[51]

One other reason for overcrowding was the disparity between government hospitals and subvented hospitals. After the war, the Hong Kong government had encouraged non-governmental organizations to establish hospitals and clinics. Over time, these institutions began to receive government financial support, which was crucial for their survival, due to the escalating cost of hospital care. Before the 1980s, these subvented hospitals provided more than half of all the hospital beds in Hong Kong. Each subvented hospital was governed by an independent board of directors and managed by a medical superintendent who oversaw hospital operations and was responsible for daily decision-making. There was little or no effective coordination between subvented hospitals and public hospitals. When a subvented hospital was full, patients were redirected to the nearest government hospital, which was forced to accept all acute and emergency cases. The government claimed that subvented hospitals offered better service and were more efficiently run, yet patients perceived them as 'second best'. Staff at these hospitals were jealous of the higher salaries enjoyed by government hospital employees doing the same work,

---

51. Robin Hutcheon, *Bedside Manners: Health and Health Care in Hong Kong*, 42.

but their morale was generally higher, chiefly because they did not have to deal with the same severe overcrowding.[52]

The government appointed Dr W. D. Scott, an Australian consultant, to conduct a review of the Medical and Health Department, with particular focus on hospitals, their organization, and their administration. In his 1985 report, Scott recommended the establishment of a statutory Hospital Authority (HA), independent of the civil service, to integrate the management structures of the hospitals, and to be funded independent of the government. The HA, the report said, should be separated from the Medical and Health Department.[53] After public consultation, the report was accepted.

In 1988, the Provisional Hospital Authority (PHA), headed by Sir S.Y. Chung, was formed to lay the groundwork, administrative and legal, for the statutory Hospital Authority to be set up in 1990.[54] Sir S. Y. was a politician and businessman who served on both the Legislative Council and the Executive Council in Hong Kong. The PHA was charged with developing proposals for a new management structure, suggesting strategies for integrating government and subvented hospitals, and constructing a legislative framework for the proposed HA.[55] Professor Young was recruited to take part in the PHA and was invited to chair the subcommittee responsible for integrating subvented and government hospitals. This was one of the PHA's most important tasks since the integration was crucial for an efficient system of hospital services.

Since subvented hospitals had their own staff, a new system that integrated their personnel with public hospitals personnel enjoying different terms of employment would have to be devised. Ownership of the properties on which subvented hospitals sat had to be discussed. Each subvented hospital had its own approach to the services it provided and its own mode of operation. All these problems would have to be solved under the new set-up.

---

52. Hutcheon, *Bedside Manners*, 39.
53. W. D. Scott, *The Delivery of Medical Service in Hospitals: A Report for the Hong Kong Government* (Hong Kong: Hong Kong Government Printers), 1985.
54. 'Can New Authority Cure Hospitals' Ills', *South China Morning Post*, 1 October 1988.
55. Hong Kong Hansard, 7 Oct 1987, 33.

Professor Young visited every one of twenty-three subvented hospitals to hold discussions. These hospitals did not wish to give up their individual characteristics to incorporate into the HA system. For example, the Tung Wah Group of Hospitals wanted all five of its hospitals to be governed together although the HA model planned for five regional committees. Tung Wah requested retaining pricing autonomy since the group provided free services for patients who needed them. In addition, the group planned to engage in its own fundraising under the future setup.[56]

After six months of meeting with the boards of the subvented hospitals, Professor Young understood their concerns. They all expressed a similar desire: they wanted to keep their own hospital boards and retain the power to hire and fire their staff. In the end, when they learned that there would be no subvention outside of the HA, all subvented hospitals agreed to integrate.[57] Professor Young and her team, for their part, convinced the new HA to allow subvented hospitals to retain their governing boards under the HA in the reorganization scheme. The HA would be represented on subvented hospital boards, and complaints could be dealt with at that level.[58]

During its fourteen months of existence, the PHA employed six firms of consultants to investigate specific issues and ensure that there would be no legal barriers to the establishment of the new HA. PHA staff spent months on difficult negotiations with government doctors and dentists over the pay package offered by the HA. The PHA made every effort to meet staff concerns and to provide an acceptable set of terms for employees. In the end, the majority of the medical and administrative staff in government and subvented hospitals signed agreements to become new HA staff.[59] The PHA also recommended management and organizational structures for the HA and its hospitals, a scheme for hospital integration, and a set of guidelines for legislation.[60]

---

56. 'PHA Plans Hospital Integration', *South China Morning Post*, 8 January 1989.
57. 'Hospitals Expected to Join New Body', *South China Morning Post*, 17 April 1990.
58. 'Hospital Boards Plan Defined', *South China Morning Post*, 13 April 1989.
59. Hutcheon, *Bedside Manners*, 97.
60. Sir S. Y. Chung, *Report of the Provisional Hospital Authority*, Hong Kong Government, December 1989.

When the Hospital Authority was formed in December 1990,[61] Professor Young was invited to be a member of the board. Hospital integration commenced in May 1991, following the blueprint prepared by the PHA. The HA gained control of all fifteen former government hospitals and twenty-three former subvented hospitals.[62] This necessitated the transfer of about 37,000 employees from twenty-four separate employers to the HA. The staff were given three years to decide whether to transfer to HA employment terms or remain on existing government or subvented terms. A great deal of work was necessary to unify sixteen different methods of paying employees, assembling staff records, and managing financial information.[63] The integration was considered a major achievement, as it was accomplished with no strikes or disruption of hospital service.[64]

Figure 5.2: Members of the First Hospital Authority Board, Sir S. Y. Chung (sitting, centre), Professor Young on his left, 1990. Source: Sir S. Y. Chung.

---

61. 《醫路──生命是美。醫院管理局二十年》（香港：香港知出版社，2012）。
62. 'Doctors Pledged on New Posts', *South China Morning Post*, 25 May 1991.
63. 《醫路──生命是美。醫院管理局二十年》，66。
64. Gauld and Gould, *The Hong Kong Health Sector*, 67–68.

On 1 April 1995, the founding chair of the HA Board, Sir S. Y. Chung, was replaced by another founding member, Mr Peter Woo. Woo, a businessman, was then the chairman of the HA Management Committee. He changed the HA into a well-managed institution. Thanks to contemporary management techniques brought to bear on a multitude of problems, the efficiency of day-to-day operations in hospitals had improved greatly. Morale had risen considerably as well.

Professor Young retired from the HA Board in 1996. She was one of the few physicians who served on both the PHA and the HA to lead the process. The establishment of the HA meant that public hospitals in Hong Kong were now on a par with those in Western countries, to the immense benefit of the patients and staff. Professor Young could be very proud of her work.

Medical Emergency Preparedness, 2003

SARS is a wake-up call for the health care system in Hong Kong. The disease, and its heavy death toll, including many health care workers, and huge economic impact, dealt an enormous blow to Hong Kong and its citizens. The silver lining, if it can be said there was one, was that Hong Kong moved to strengthen its preparedness for future medical disasters.

The disease originated in South China in November 2002. One of the affected patients, a doctor from Guangzhou, arrived in Hong Kong on 21 February.[65] During his stay in a hotel, he infected several guests lodging on the same floor of the hotel.[66] From Hong Kong, an international city, the disease spread rapidly to several countries. By the time the SARS epidemic was over, 8,096 individuals had been infected worldwide, and 774 had died from the disease. In Hong Kong, there were 1,755 cases and 299

---

65. Epidemiologic Clues to SARS Origin in China, accessed 29 August 2023, https://www.ncbi.nlm.nih.gov/pmc/articles/PMC3323155/.
66. 'This Hotel Is Infamous as Ground Zero for a SARS "Super Spreader" in the 2003 Outbreak', accessed 29 August 2023, https://www.cnbc.com/2020/02/14/hong-kong-hotel-hosted-super-spreader-in-the-2003-sars-outbreak.html.

deaths.[67] There were several post-SARS initiatives to examine what had gone wrong in Hong Kong and what could be done better in the future. The most significant one was the SARS Expert Committee, composed of experts in health care, epidemiology, statistics, infectious diseases, and hospital management. All of these experts were invited from overseas with the exception of two, and Professor Young was one of them. Every aspect of the SARS outbreak was scrutinized.[68]

The committee found that the severity of the epidemic in Hong Kong might have been lessened had accurate data about this atypical pneumonia been available to the Hong Kong government or the international community as the outbreak unfolded in Guangdong Province. The expert panel reassured the people of Hong Kong that authorities had acted reasonably, given the information they had at the time. Beyond highlighting the lessons learned, the committee made several recommendations for future outbreak preparedness, based on common principles of public health emergencies, as follows:[69]

(1) Formation of a Centre for Health Protection within the Department of Health with the goal of achieving effective prevention and control of diseases in Hong Kong;

(2) Closer collaboration with the Pearl River Delta region, China, and with the international community;

(3) Coordination within Hong Kong to achieve better working relationships between the Department of Health, the Hospital Authority, the universities, and the private sector;

(4) Improvement in the management of an epidemic, including surge capacity in intensive care beds, staffing, appropriate provision for care of patients, laboratory capacity, supplies, personal

---

67. The World Health Organization based on data ending December 2003, 'Summary of Probable SARS Cases with Onset of Illness from 1 November 2002 to 31 July 2003', accessed 1 March 2023, https://www.who.int/publications/m/item/summary-of-probable-sars-cases-with-onset-of-illness-from-1-november-2002-to-31-july-2003.
68. *SARS Expert Committee Report*, 85–119.
69. *SARS Expert Committee Report*, 65–72.

protective equipment, etc. A clear chain of command and control should be established in response to an epidemic;
(5) Establishment of more effective, transparent communication between different institutions and, more importantly, communication to the public as an outbreak unfolds;
(6) Strengthening of the surveillance systems for early detection, reporting, and data management; and
(7) Initiation of research and training.

The *SARS Expert Committee Report* was accepted by the government, and Professor Young was appointed to the Committee on Implementation of the Recommendations of the Expert Committee. The Centre for Health Protection was set up in 2004. An existing surveillance program was expanded to include a network of more than forty private general practitioners and sixty-four public-sentinel general outpatient clinics for acute infectious diseases.[70] A Health Research Council was formed for the first time in the history of Hong Kong. Professor Young sat on the committee from 2003 to 2009 to evaluate the research grant proposals.

Professor Young had a close encounter with SARS. In 2003, she was invited by the Hong Kong Medical Council to chair the Visiting Team for the Review of Education and Training in the University of Hong Kong and the Chinese University of Hong Kong. On 10 March 2003, when the team arrived at Ward 8A, Prince of Wales Hospital, they were directed to a different ward on another floor. That morning, eleven health care staff including doctors and nurses, and several medical students who took their examination in Ward 8A on the previous day, had all suddenly fallen ill from a mysterious disease. It was fortunate that the team was directed away from Ward 8A, as it housed one of the major foci for the spread of SARS in Hong Kong.

Hong Kong had learned its lessons from SARS, and the 2008–2009 swine flu outbreak was quickly brought under control. This time medical professionals did everything right. The disease was deemed 'notifiable'

---

70. Moira M. W. Chan-Yeung, *A Medical History of Hong Kong: The Development and Contributions of Outpatient Clinics* (Hong Kong: Chinese University of Hong Kong Press, 2022), 123–24.

as soon as it hit the territory. Preventive measures were carried out in all institutions according to the protocol developed after the SARS outbreak. The moment the virus was confirmed in an individual, the Department of Health ordered contact tracing, and when contacts were identified, they were quarantined. Infected patients were sent to specifically designated hospitals. There was daily communication with the public, including direct messaging from the chief executive. The swine flu infected 32,301 people. Fortunately, the disease was mild. There was no panic or fear in the city. Hong Kong had passed the test of emergency preparedness.[71]

Hong Kong responded with satisfactory results to the first four waves of the recent COVID-19 pandemic. When the fifth wave struck on 31 December 2021, because of the high infectivity of Omicron, a new variant of the COVID-19 virus that had many mutations, the number of new cases each day rose very quickly and reached around 55,000 at its peak.[72] Hospitals were overwhelmed because of the large number of severe cases. The death rate in Hong Kong from this wave of COVID-19 was said to be one of the highest in the world among the elderly who had not been fully vaccinated.[73] There will certainly be post-mortems on the COVID-19 pandemic when it is over. Hong Kong will learn more lessons from this prolonged episode.

Hospital Boards

In addition to her other public service responsibilities, Professor Young served on the board of Prince Philip Dental Hospital from 1981 to 1988 and of Princess Margaret Hospital from 1992 to 1996. The world-class dental hospital was opened by its namesake, Prince Philip, then chairman of the British Dental Association. Professor Young, dean of HKU's Faculty of Medicine at the time, helped in the curriculum development and other

---

71. Chan-Yeung, *A Medical History of Hong Kong, 1942–2015*, 163–65.
72. Latest Situation of COVID-19, Centre for Health Protection Hong Kong, accessed 3 October 2022, https://www.chp.gov.hk/files/pdf/local_situation_covid19_en.pdf.
73. Luke Taylor, 'Covid-19: Hong Kong Reports World's Highest Death Rate as Zero Covid Strategy Fails', *British Medical Journal*, 2022, accessed 16 February 2023, https://www.bmj.com/content/bmj/376/bmj.o707.full.pdf.

clinical matters. The first cohort of dental students graduated in 1985, easing the critical shortage of dentists in Hong Kong. In 2016, the HKU Faculty of Dentistry was ranked number one in the world, according to QS World University Rankings,[74] and it remained second between 2017 and 2022. The school is exceptional because of the culture of research among the faculty and students.

Princess Margaret Hospital, a major regional hospital in the Kwai Chung area, was opened in October 1975, by Princess Margaret. In 1990, after the establishment of the Hospital Authority, individual hospitals had permission to raise funds locally for the development of special projects. As a board member, Professor Young encouraged the hospital to find a project that would ultimately give it a niche in Hong Kong. Princess Margaret Hospital had taken her advice and became a tertiary referral centre for infectious diseases, nephrology, and urology and is now one of the teaching hospitals in Hong Kong to provide training for interns and residents. The staff are unusually loyal, and they invariably return to serve the hospital after training at other centres, locally or overseas, despite good offers from elsewhere.

Her Contributions to Medicine and Medical Education

A compassionate and highly competent physician, Professor Young benefited the thousands of patients she attended. She pioneered the Endocrinology and Metabolic Diseases Unit at Queen Mary Hospital and turned it into a major clinical and research centre. She trained all the sub-specialists in the discipline during that era.

Her work with the Hong Kong Medical Council resulted in an enlarged and more democratic Medical Council with representation from laypeople and ensured a higher professional standard and patient protection. Through the Working Party on Primary Health Care, she helped lay the principles of the much-needed primary health care reforms. The current reforms in primary care are based on the same principles as in the

---

74. 'Hong Kong Tops World Ranking of Dental Schools', *Hong Kong Economic Journal*, 22 March 2016.

WPPHC. She was actively involved in the establishment of the Hospital Authority with extensive reforms leading to much better in-patient care. Her vast experience in medicine and administration placed her in the SARS Expert Committee to improve Hong Kong's preparedness in response to medical disasters and on the subsequent committee to ensure the implementation of the recommendations of the Expert Committee. Her public service activities covered almost every important aspect of medical and health care in Hong Kong—outpatient and inpatient medical care, and public health—and in medical education. The reforms in health care resulted in an efficient and high standard medical workforce, an improved health care system, and a healthier population whose life expectancy has ranked consistently one of the highest in the world. Very few physicians in the history of Hong Kong can match Professor Young in her contributions to medicine in Hong Kong.

6

Mentor to Leader

Public Service in Education

New Direction

If research was in Professor McFadzean's blood, then teaching was in Professor Rosie Young's. Her father's effectiveness as teacher and tutor allowed her to complete her secondary education in only three years before her admission to HKU. As a child, playing school, being the teacher was Professor Young's favourite pastime. From the time she was teaching young doctors she had a persistent piece of advice for them: make sure you pass on your knowledge to the next generation so that they are better than you are.

As a teacher, Professor Young stressed the importance of principles and promoted clear, logical thinking rather than rote recall. While Old Mac was respected and dreaded, Professor Young was admired yet never feared. Like her mentor, however, she required medical students to be neatly dressed and presentable as doctors, to command the necessary respect. She had no hesitation in reminding her students or juniors to cut their hair when necessary. Endowed with a sharp, clear voice that could be readily heard at the back of the room, she had a distinct advantage over others—a blessing indeed in the classroom and in presentations or debates.

Given her love of teaching and her mission to pass on knowledge, it is not surprising that Professor Young took up public service in education. Her involvement began in 1987 with her appointment as a member of the Hong Kong Examination Authority (renamed Hong Kong Examinations and Assessment Authority in 2002), a statutory body responsible for the administration of public examinations and related assessments. By 1993, when she was invited to take over the chairmanship of the Education Commission, Professor Young had been following the progress of public education in Hong Kong for many years.

Many families in Hong Kong in the late 1940s and 1950s were poor, and schooling was costly. Girls were considered secondary, and from a young age they took on the care of younger siblings and helped with household chores while both parents worked long hours for their sons' education. As the economy in Hong Kong improved and wages increased, families who could afford it sent their boys to university while their girls were expected to leave school after the School Certificate Examination and find work to help support their younger brothers. The 1966 and 1967 riots in Hong Kong forced the government to reform. As the economy advanced, by 1971, it completed implementation of compulsory, free six-year primary education for children aged six to twelve. This meant that all girls in Hong Kong received at least primary education from then on.

The government produced two White Papers on educational reform, in 1974 and 1978, both published after extensive consultation with the public. The main aim of the 1974 White Paper on *Secondary Education Over the Next Decade* was to provide three years of free junior secondary education for all boys and girls in the 12–14 age group, and sufficient places in senior secondary forms for at least 40 per cent of the 15–16 age group by 1979.[1] The government actually managed to implement this policy in 1978, one year early. The 1978 White Paper on the *Development of Senior Secondary and Tertiary Education* proposed the provision of subsidized senior secondary places for 60 per cent of the fifteen-year-old

---

1. White Paper, *Secondary Education in Hong Kong Over the Next Decade*, tabled in the Legislative Council, 16 October 1975, Hong Kong Government, accessed 23 February 2023, https://www.eduhk.hk/cird/publications/edpolicy/02.pdf.

population by 1981, rising to more than 70 per cent by 1986. In addition, teacher education was to be strengthened, school curriculum enriched, and facilities and support services to schools improved.[2] During this period, five technical institutes were built and equipped, offering a wide range of disciplines. Professor Young, who had been following the issue closely, watched with satisfaction as girls began to enjoy the same educational opportunities as boys. In her own family, thanks to her parents, that had always been the case.

In 1981, the government invited the visiting Organisation for Economic and Co-operation Development (OECD) Education Panel to conduct an overall review of Hong Kong education following three decades of expansion. The four-member review panel was headed by Sir John Llewellyn. They visited Hong Kong twice and toured schools, universities, the Hong Kong Polytechnic, technical institutes, a college of education, and a post-secondary college. In addition, they reviewed numerous written representations from the public and private educational groups, and former policies and background material. The long-awaited report, known as the Llewellyn Report, was published in November 1982.[3] The panel called for a complete overhaul of the education system, including the power structure of education policy-making, which included the establishment of an education commission (EC) to advise the government on all matters relating to education and education policy and to coordinate the development of education at different levels.[4]

The EC under Sir Quo Wei Lee began to consider the other major proposals in the report, including the controversial one on the shift towards use of mother tongue as medium of instruction (MOI) in schools.[5] This issue dominated the EC reports in the subsequent years. Between 1984 and 1997, the EC published seven reports (ECRs 1–7), focusing on

---

2. *The Development of Senior Secondary and Tertiary Education in Hong Kong*, October 1978, Hong Kong Government, accessed 23 February 2023, https://www.eduhk.hk/cird/publications/edpolicy/04.pdf.
3. Anthony Sweeting, *Educational History of Hong Kong 1941–2001: Visions and Revisions* (Hong Kong: Hong Kong University Press, 2004), 339.
4. Sweeting, *Education in Hong Kong 1941 to 2001*, 366.
5. 'LegCo Split on Report', *South China Morning Post*, 13 July 1983.

improving the quality of education. Reports 1 through 6 covered language teaching and learning, teacher quality, private sector school improvements, curriculum development, teaching and learning conditions, and special education.[6] The seventh report, ECR-7, was published in 1997, after the establishment of the HKSAR. Professor Young was responsible for the preparation and publication of ECR-6 and ECR-7.

The Education Commission, 1993–1997

By 1993, when professor Young became chair of the EC, she had considerable experience with chairing committees. Her job this time was not so straightforward, however. The twenty-one members of the EC, experts and professionals from the educational sector, fell roughly into three groups: pro-democrats, pro-establishment, and pro-China. Since the groups had opposing views on many subjects, every issue was discussed at length, and decision-making was slow. Some newly appointed members also required an orientation to the workings of the EC. Delay in obtaining data and reports from the Education Department meant some decisions and discussions of major areas had to be postponed.

A few months into Professor Young's appointment as chair, two members of the EC, Professor Arthur Li and Dr Paul Morris, resigned suddenly. The two men called a press conference on 13 November 1993, at which they stated, 'This decision [to resign] has been taken because we believe the commission now lacks a clear sense of direction and purpose which is in marked contrast to its earlier role. Critical policy areas, such as Special and Pre-primary education, which have been identified by members as topics the commission should focus on, have been ignored ... The goal seems to turn the commission into a "talking shop" that does not address any major policy issues which have resource implications.'[7]

---

6. Yin Cheong Cheng, 'Hong Kong Educational Reforms in the Last Decade: Reform Syndrome and New Developments', *International Journal of Educational Management* 23, no. 1 (2009): 65–86.

7. 'Two Quit "Useless" Education Policy Body', *South China Morning Post*, 13 November 1993.

In a later interview, the two former members of the EC charged that the commission had become little more than a rubber stamp to approve government policy, the Education Department deciding which direction the group should take.[8] Because some of the EC's past proposals had been quite expensive, they believed that the government was trying to steer the commission into addressing marginal topics rather than major policy issues. The two emphasized that they were not mounting a personal attack on Professor Young. They realized that Professor Young was an academic and not a politician, so it was a disadvantage from that point of view. Her two predecessors, Sir Quo Wei Lee and Mrs Rita Fan Hsu Lai Tai, had been executive councillors and more used to forging alliances between different groups. Dr Morris also added, 'It is extremely difficult for her [Professor Young] if you do have an agenda which has been strongly manipulated by the government, so she has an extremely difficult task.' The two former members of the EC directed their attacks not at her but at the government.

At the time Professor Li spoke to the press, he was the chairman of the Department of Surgery at CUHK and a member of the Hong Kong Medical Council representing CUHK. Professor Young was still chairing the Medical Council then. Professor Li was known for his demanding and aggressive style, often engaging in heated arguments during Medical Council meetings. Dr Paul Morris, an internationally renowned educational scholar, was dean of HKU's Faculty of Education from 1986 to 1992 and HKU's chair professor in curriculum studies in 1997. By 1993, he had served on the EC for five years.

When Professor Young heard the news, she was devastated. Even though Professors Li and Dr Morris had not called on her to resign, she felt that she would need to step down. However, several events occurred in the next few days. First, HKU Vice-Chancellor Wang Gungwu called Professor Young, comforted her, and urged her not to resign. Second, Michael Leung, the secretary for the Education and Manpower Branch and vice-chairman of the EC, told Professor Young that there was no point in resigning, and promised to help her. But what finally swayed her was a

---

8. 'Education Group "Sidelined"', *South China Morning Post*, 17 November 1993.

letter from Governor Chris Patten, who encouraged her to carry on. If she did well in the future despite difficulties, he said, she would be very much appreciated and would prove the two ex-members wrong.

On 16 November, Professor Young, in a press interview, admitted that there was 'substance' in the allegations by the two ex-members that the EC had become a 'talking shop'. She denied that the EC lacked a sense of direction and purpose, but admitted that, on occasion, members had spent too little time discussing substantive topics. Too much time had been spent on procedural matters, she said, especially on the issue of confidentiality. She explained also that many members were new to the commission. She told the press: 'I myself and other Education Commission members have learned this lesson, and this is an important lesson and this matter is now behind us because the procedural matters have been more or less resolved.'[9]

In the same interview, Professor Young announced that the EC would embark on major studies in three areas: language proficiency, educational standards, and resource allocation. She believed that these studies would have long-lasting implications for the future of education of Hong Kong. She also decided she would give a press conference herself after each EC meeting to inform the media about what had been on the agenda and any decisions that had been made. This would make the EC more transparent and more open to the public. Professor Young had always believed in transparency, and by taking this approach, she also dealt effectively with the criticism that EC lacked focus.

She nominated Dr Cheng Kai Ming, a staff member of the Faculty of Education, HKU, as one of the replacements for the two members who resigned. He would play a far more significant role in the EC after Professor Young stepped down in 1998. Two more new members were added to the commission as well: Sansan Ching, director of the Hong Kong Council of Early Childhood Education and Services (CECES),[10] and Peter Lee Ting-chang, director of Lee Hysan Estate Co. Ltd. Sansan

---

9. 'Education Chief Accepts Criticism', *South China Morning Post*, 16 November 1993.
10. Hong Kong Council of Early Childhood Education, accessed 23 February 2023, https://hkceces.org/en/about-ceces-en/.

Ching, an expert in early childhood education, had founded CECES, an organization that published readers, created learning materials for the primary school English curriculum, and helped create an electronic education platform for preschool children, teachers, and parents.[11] A pre-primary education project had been on the agenda of EC for a while but had yet to be discussed, so her appointment to the commission should have been timely. However, the research showing that major brain growth and development take place between the ages of zero and five years was not yet widely known, and regrettably, the EC did not consider compulsory and free pre-primary education a priority.

Resignation is a decision no one takes lightly, particularly from an important government commission. However, at times it is the most effective way of making a point. After the resignation of the two EC members, some members exhibited more willingness to be constructive and to yield on minor points. Professor Young received tremendous help from the vice-chairman of the EC, Michael Leung, who was the secretary for the Education and Manpower Branch then. Leung paid personal attention to ensure that important issues were on the agenda and that the relevant data required were ready on time for meetings. He also suggested the points to pass along to the press. Since then, a great deal of work was accomplished, resulting in the publication of two influential reports, ECR-6 and ECR-7.

Education Commission Report 6, 1996

The EC had decided in 1993 that language proficiency would be one of the major areas of investigation. The MOI had been an issue in Hong Kong for a long time. The only university in Hong Kong after the war, HKU, taught in English. Most of the secondary schools labelled themselves as Anglo-Chinese schools using English as MOI, and they prepared students for HKU or universities overseas. The rest of the schools in Hong Kong used Chinese as their MOI. Before the war, graduates from Chinese schools usually went to China for their higher education. Despite the closure of

---

11. Sansan Ching, accessed 23 February 2023, https://hk.linkedin.com/in/sansan-ching-2463a6ab.

the border between Hong Kong and China in 1951, students continued to go into China and some also left for Taiwan to further their studies. In 1963, the Chinese University of Hong Kong (CUHK) was founded to offer students greater opportunity for higher education locally. While most of the courses were taught in Chinese, the professional faculties, such as medicine, law, engineering, and accountancy, which were added later, used English in instruction.

The establishment of CUHK was accompanied by a growing awareness of the importance of the Chinese language, if Hong Kong, a city where East meets West, was to establish a meaningful relationship with China and to realize its dream as a world city. Increasing awareness of national identity among local residents was accompanied by a heightened demand for wider use of the Chinese language in Hong Kong. In 1965, the Hong Kong Federation of Students organized a symposium in Chung Chi College of CUHK on improving post-secondary education in Hong Kong. One of the topics discussed was the inclusion of Chinese language as one of the two official languages in Hong Kong, which received enthusiastic support from many participants.[12]

After the riots of 1966 and 1967, in January of 1968, students from Chung Chi College organized a meeting and invited representatives from other tertiary institutions to discuss the inclusion of Chinese as an official language in Hong Kong. This was followed in July 1970 by a symposium to discuss the establishment by ordinance of the Chinese language as one of the official languages.[13] In September 1970, the government set up a Chinese Language Committee. By 1974, the Official Languages Ordinance was enacted, to include the Chinese language as the second official language in communication between the government institutions and the general public.[14]

---

12. 馮以浤，〈學運的歷史意義及評價〉，載香港專上學生聯會編，《香港學生運動回顧》（香港：廣角鏡出版社，1983），297。
13. 馮以浤，〈學運的歷史意義及評價〉，297–98。
14. Ping Chen, 'Language Policy in Hong Kong during the Colonial Period before July 1 1997', in *Language Planning and Language Policy: East Asian Perspectives*, ed. Ping Chen and Nanette Gottlieb (Cornwall: Curzon Press, 2001), 111–28.

However, the situation in schools was different in the 1960s and 1970s. The expansion of education in Hong Kong resulted in more students prepared for senior secondary and university education. The number of schools using English as their MOI increased considerably since most parents wanted their children to become professionals such as doctors, lawyers, engineers, and accountants. In these professions, English was the dominant language. In many so-called Anglo-Chinese schools using English as MOI, although the textbooks used were in English, instruction was carried out in Cantonese. There were two main reasons for this: there was a shortage of trained teachers to teach all subjects in English, and students might not be able to understand English, especially those in junior secondary schools, as most of the Form 1 (Secondary 1) students came from Chinese primary schools. As a result, both English and Chinese were used as languages of instruction in these schools. This practice, although acceptable to most parents, was considered undesirable by many, including the Hong Kong government.[15]

In 1973, the government, in view of the growing importance of the Chinese language, introduced a Green Paper, which recommended using Chinese as MOI in junior secondary classes.[16] In the White Paper *Secondary Education in Hong Kong Over the Next Decade* that followed in 1974, however, the decision of MOI was left to schools themselves.[17]

The Llewellyn Report published in 1982 proposed that Cantonese be adopted as the MOI up to the junior secondary level because only a small group of elite students benefited from using English in these grades. After the Sino-British Joint Declaration was signed in 1984, Chinese-medium instruction was further promoted as the policy in the ECRs. However, strong opposition from the public forced the government to change its mind again to adopt a policy of leaving the choice of MOI

---

15. Joseph Boyle, 'Hong Kong's Educational System: English or Chinese?', *Language, Culture and Curriculum* 8, no. 3 (1995): 291–302.
16. 許寶強，〈母語教育與情感政治——香港的大學和中學授課語言的文化研究〉，accessed 12 March 2023, https://www.thinkinghk.org/v605.
17. White Paper, *Secondary Education in Hong Kong Over the Next Decade*, accessed 12 March 2023, https://www.eduhk.hk/cird/publications/edpolicy/02.pdf.

to school principals.[18] By 1992, 90 per cent of secondary schools had chosen English as their MOI. In primary schools, 90 per cent had chosen Chinese, since their students had difficulty understanding English.[19] Over the same period, classroom instruction, which was actually using English in instruction in Anglo-Chinese schools, decreased from 43 per cent in the 1980s to 15 per cent in the 1990s,[20] as a result of universal education for nine years, which enabled students with lower scholastic achievement to enter secondary schools. This situation aroused concern from educators and government officials. In 1990–1991, an international study was carried out comparing the level of reading literacy achieved by students in the 'first' languages of a number of education systems for the Evaluation of Educational Achievement.[21] The results of the study were presented in 1993 and published in 1994. The standard of English of Hong Kong students at the Secondary 3 level was found to be low—a disturbing finding because the students tested were in their third year of English-medium education.[22]

Under Professor Young as EC chairman, a working group was formed to investigate the problem related to language proficiency in October 1993. The group, led by Professor Young, visited a number of local schools as well as schools in Belgium and the Netherlands. These two countries were chosen because they were non-English speaking, multilingual, and multiracial, similar to Hong Kong. She and her colleagues were impressed by the success in these two countries. Based on their findings, the working group recommended that young children in Hong Kong be taught in their mother tongue first, the second language to be introduced after the age of eight. The two countries chosen, though similar to Hong Kong in

---

18. Kingsley Bolton, 'Hong Kong English: Autonomy and Creativity', in *Hong Kong English: Autonomy and Creativity*, ed. Kingsley Bolton (Hong Kong: Hong Kong University Press, 2002), 1–5.
19. Boyle, 'Hong Kong's Educational System', 291–302.
20. Joseph Boyle, 'English in Hong Kong', *English Today* 13, no. 2 (1997): 3–6.
21. 'Reading Literacy Study International Association for the Evaluation of Educational Achievement', accessed 13 March 2023, https://nap.nationalacademies.org/read/9174/chapter/15.
22. 'Low English Standard Disturbing', *South China Morning Post*, 2 March 1994.

their multiracial aspects, are quite different in other aspects. The origin of Dutch, French, German, and English is the same, and they are similar. It is not uncommon for two or three languages to be used at home, and children are exposed to several languages when they are young. English is an entirely different language from Chinese. It is more difficult for Chinese to learn, and in most families, exposure to English is uncommon. It might be more appropriate to study the situation in Singapore, where different languages spoken include English, Chinese, Malay, and Tamil.

In July 1994, the Working Group published a draft report for a three-month public consultation. In the light of public response to the report, the EC produced a draft ECR-6, entitled *Enhancing Language Proficiency: A Comprehensive Strategy*, for more public consultation in mid-December 1995 over a period of six weeks. The commission conducted twenty-nine briefing sessions for legislators, educators, teachers' unions, business and employer associations, professional bodies, representatives from different types of schools, parents, and the media. It generated a great deal of public interest and discussion. It was the subject of over 120 editorials, articles in all the major Chinese and English newspapers, and 155 written submissions from educational organizations and members of the public. At the time, more than 90 per cent of children went to kindergartens in Hong Kong where English was also taught. Most of the teachers were not qualified to teach English because, as noted, there was a shortage of qualified English teachers in Hong Kong.[23] Nonetheless, the general opinion expressed in the media was that late introduction of English was something no parent would accept. Nor would any kindergarten be brave enough to stop teaching English, because their survival depended on enrolment, and they knew how parents would react. The Working Group's recommendations were indeed met with strong opposition from parents.[24]

---

23. C. K. Lau, 'Brave New World of Language Education', *South China Morning Post*, 16 July 1994.
24. Lau, 'Brave New World of Language Education'.

The final report was published in March 1996.²⁵ It is not surprising that the EC did not change but reaffirmed the MOI policy of ECR-4.²⁶ Realizing how poorly English had been taught in schools, ECR-6 also made major recommendations to improve on the teaching of English: (1) to improve teacher education and training and, a controversial one—to benchmark the qualifications of language teachers; (2) to determine realistic language proficiency goals for different levels of education; and (3) to establish a Standing Committee on Language Education and Research (SCOLAR) composed of language experts, educators, and other stakeholders, to formulate, monitor, and evaluate language policy.²⁷ There were a number of other recommendations. Interested readers can access the report directly from the website indicated in note 25.

In 1994, the Hong Kong government set up a $300 million fund to improve language proficiency. The Language Fund Advisory Committee was established to determine the funding criteria and vet applications. Professor Young was appointed chair. In the vetting process, she was assisted by Mrs Elim Lau, headmistress of the Diocesan Girls' School, for the English submissions, and Mr Szeto Wah, a primary school principal, founder of the Hong Kong Professional Teachers' Union and member of the Legislative Council of Hong Kong, for the Chinese submissions.

After the establishment of the HKSAR in 1997, individual secondary schools were told whether they should use English or Chinese as their MOI according to the level of achievement of students in English entering Secondary 1. The policy was strictly reinforced. Implementation prompted unprecedented reactions from the public and caused widespread fear and confusion about first-language education. Most parents resented the

---

25. *Education Commission Report No. 6, Enhancing Language Proficiency: A Comprehensive Strategy*, March 1996, Education Bureau, Hong Kong Government, accessed 23 February 2023, https://www.e-c.edu.hk/doc/en/publications_and_related_documents/education_reports/ecr6_e.pdf.
26. *Education Commission Report No. 4*, 1990, Education Bureau, Hong Kong Government, accessed 7 July 2020, https://www.edb.gov.hk/attachment/en/curriculum-development/major-level-of-edu/gifted/hong-kong-development/ecr4_e.pdf.
27. Standing Committee on Language Education and Research (SCOLAR), accessed 23 February 2023, https://scolarhk.edb.hkedcity.net/en/about-scolar-introduction.

policy. Schools saw it as socially divisive, taking away their autonomy, and in the schools that were instructed to change their MOI from English to Chinese, 66 per cent of principals thought their schools were now marked as second class because of the change. The business sector feared that the reduced exposure to English for students would compromise the city's competitiveness and status as an international centre.[28] All these anxieties indicate that language in education policy is more than a school issue; it is also a social issue. However, by 2020, all schools were following the government policy. Academically, it would be of interest to see whether the decline in English proficiency among Hong Kong students has been arrested.

Education Commission Report No. 7, 1997

In the 1950s, the Hong Kong government faced a tumultuous political situation generated by the founding of the Communist Party's People's Republic of China. It began to exert strong central control over schools and school curriculum, except for pro-communist private schools, to ensure that they were not used to destabilize the colonial government. It was also an era of mass education, which was an expensive item on the budget. The government wanted uniformity and accountability and controlled school spending with rules and regulations of the Grant Code and the Subsidy Code. A highly centralized system emerged, in which each student's progress through the stages of schooling was determined by their performance on highly competitive public examinations. Teacher involvement in curriculum development was restricted because the government controlled the key elements, including content, textbooks, and examinations.[29]

Since the early 1990s, school-based management (SBM) to improve the quality of education had been used in about 25,000 schools in the

---

28. Wei Zeng, 'Medium of Instruction in Secondary Education in Post-colonial Hong Kong: Why Chinese? Why English?', *Working Papers in Educational Linguistics* 22 (2007): 42–56.
29. Paul Morris and Bob Adamson, *Curriculum, Schooling and Society in Hong Kong* (Hong Kong: Hong Kong University Press, 2010), 31–33.

UK; Canada, Australia, New Zealand, and the US followed suit. SBM is the systematic decentralization to the school level of authority to make decisions on significant matters related to operations within a centrally determined framework of goals, policies, curriculum, standards, and accountability.[30] Hong Kong schools needed to join the international trend to have more autonomy and less control centrally. There had been some reforms in Hong Kong schools related to decentralization, such as school-based curriculum and a school management initiative (SMI), to encourage schools to take greater responsibility in decision making, but more decentralization was necessary for SBM to be implemented. Due to her experience of the devolution of tasks from central administration to faculty level as a pro-vice-chancellor at HKU, Professor Young was highly in favour of SBM.

It is necessary to measure the effects of changes in policy on the quality of education. Quality benchmarks are necessary. In November 1993, Professor Young announced that education standards and resource allocation would be the two major areas of study for ECR-7. She set up a Working Group on Educational Standards and a Quality Assurance Unit of about twenty professionals to visit a number of schools and kindergartens each year.[31] Based on the results of these studies, in April 1996, the EC set up a Task Group on School Quality and School Funding. The Task Group conducted two public consultation exercises: one in June 1996 to seek views on quality and funding issues and another one in November on proposals to improve school performance and school management. The ECR-7 was completed and published in September 1997—the first report published after the establishment of the Hong Kong SAR.[32]

---

30. Brian Caldwell, *School-Based Management*, Educational Policy Series, International Academy of Learning and International Institute of Educational Planning, 2005, UNESCO Digital Library, accessed 16 February 2023, https://unesdoc.unesco.org/ark:/48223/pf0000141025.
31. 'Educators Told Set Standards', *South China Morning Post*, 8 December 1994.
32. *Education Commission Report No. 7, Quality School Education*, September 1997, Education Bureau, Hong Kong Government, accessed 23 February 2023, https://www.e-c.edu.hk/doc/en/publications_and_related_documents/education_reports/ecr7_e_2.pdf.

ECR-7 concluded that there was a need to help schools improve their performance and to ensure that the resources devoted to school education are deployed in the most effective, efficient, and accountable manner. The EC therefore formulated recommendations mainly focusing on ways to improve school management and performance towards the provision of quality school education to better meet the needs of students.[33] The five main recommendations were: (1) to develop quality indicators to assess the performance of schools and provide incentive for schools to make continuous improvement; (2) to put in place an internal quality assurance system that included SBM and self-evaluation by schools as well as an external quality assurance mechanism, such as periodic inspection of schools by the ED; (3) to provide flexibility in the use of resources under a clear management and accountability system to schools that practise SBM; (4) to set up a Quality Education Development Fund supported and managed by the Education Department, to encourage bottom-up initiatives; (5) to promote a pre-service and in-service training strategy for teachers and to establish a fair and open performance assessment system for principals and teachers in all schools; and (6) to establish a General Teaching Council to enhance the standards of teaching and the professional development of teachers.

However, for these recommendations to be fully effective, some steps had to be taken: (1) devolution by the government of more responsibility to the schools regarding daily operations, resource management, and planning for development; (2) development of SBM to best meet the needs of schools and students; and (3) a review of the curriculum and examination system.[34]

During the preparation of ECR-7, Professor Young experienced a challenging incident. In 1995, members of the EC expressed an interest in visiting China to learn about its education system. However, there was a problem of obtaining a visa from the government of China for one of the members, and the planned official visit was called off.[35] Among some

---

33. *Education Commission Report No. 7.*
34. *Education Commission Report No. 7.*
35. 'Activists Not Welcome in China', *South China Morning Post*, 6 August 1995.

members of the EC, including Professor Young, the desire to gain more information about education in China was so strong that they decided to go privately and pay for the tour out of their own pockets. At the border, these members were surprised by a huge banner of welcome from China and the presence of Chinese news media. They were treated as an official delegation. The members learned a great deal about education in China during this visit. Newspapers in China and Hong Kong alike carried the news of their visit prominently. On their return to Hong Kong, these members were met by the press at the airport. As chairman of the EC, Professor Young was very embarrassed.

In 1998, Professor Young stepped down as chairman of the EC, and she was succeeded by Mr Antony K. C. Leung, who had a background in economics and statistics and was not an educator or an educationalist. He had a great ambition to carry out a complete overhaul in education within a short time, in contrast to Professor Young's policy of carrying out reforms in stages. A large number of reforms were implemented in succession and with rapidity. The Education and Manpower Bureau organized courses, seminars, and workshops so that teachers could obtain the necessary knowledge and skills to implement planned changes in many areas, such as school-based curriculum, school-based assessment, school management initiatives, school self-evaluation, language proficiency for English-medium instruction, new curriculum subjects, Putonghua teaching, use of information technology in teaching, and learning and management.

The seemingly endless increase in professional development activities and training sessions soon became a serious burden for teachers. Suffering from stress and fatigue, some teachers resigned.[36] The Hong Kong Institute of Education offered workshops and conferences on professional development days, and there was one on 'Teacher Burn Out'[37] but this regrettably failed to prevent two teachers from committing suicide

---

36. Cheng, 'Hong Kong Educational Reforms in the Last Decade, 75–76.
37. Cheng, 'Hong Kong Educational Reforms in the Last Decade', 76.

in 2006.[38] Realizing the serious repercussions the reforms were having on the mental health of teachers, the government established a committee to investigate the causes and recommend solutions. After the new secretary for education was appointed, the speed of education reform was slowed down, and the working conditions for teachers were improved, such as smaller classes and increased salaries.[39]

The attitude of the government with a top-down approach in executing the reforms and the rapid pace of development and implementation of the proposals led many to question whether these policies have been executed effectively.[40] There is at least one study showing the difficulties of accomplishing the self-evaluation programme in Hong Kong schools.[41] The impact of most of these policies has yet to be fully analysed.[42]

Other Public Services in Education

Serving as chairman of the EC had taught Professor Young a great deal, including how to deal with government bureaucrats and politicians and how to handle the press. After she stepped down, she was often asked by the government to chair other committees, e.g., the second round of the Teaching and Learning Quality Process Review (TLQPR) Panel for Tertiary Institutions in Hong Kong.

After her retirement from HKU in 1999, Professor Young remained active in the field of education. She served as a member of the Board of Trustees for the Jardine Scholarships; the Board of Admission, Chevening

---

38. 'Teachers Protest following Stress-Related Suicides', *Education International*, 23 January 2006, accessed 23 February 2023, https://www.ei-ie.org/en/detail/54/hong-kong-teachers-protest-following-stress-related-suicides.
39. Cheng, 'Hong Kong Educational Reforms in the Last Decade', 81–82.
40. 曾榮光，《香港教育政策分析》（香港：三聯書店香港有限公司），2011，x。
41. Nicholas Sun-Keung Pang, 'The Quality Assurance Movement: Lessons from Hong Kong Schools', in *New Challenges in Education: Lessons from Around the World* (Sofia: Bulgarian Comparative Education Society Conference Books, 2021), vol. 19, 83–90.
42. Yin Cheong Cheng and Wai Ming Cheung, 'Analysing Hong Kong Educational Policy: Application of a Comprehensive Framework', in *Handbook in Educational Policy in Hong Kong (1965–1998)* (Hong Kong: Hong Kong Institute of Education), 1998.

Scholarship, British Council; the Awardee Selection Committee, Innovation & Technology Scholarship, HKSAR, and other organizations. At the time of writing, she is a member and deputy chairman of the Executive Committee of the Friends of Cambridge University in Hong Kong, an organization that administers the Prince Philip Scholarship for students to study at Cambridge. She was a founding member of the Chinese Foundation Secondary School, serving as chairman of its School Management Committee since 2005. In addition, she accepted a number of appointments from universities in China and from various professional organizations locally and overseas (Appendix 1).

A firm believer in giving mature individuals a second chance at higher education, Professor Young enthusiastically supported the establishment of the Open Learning Institute of Hong Kong, founded in 1989 by the government. The institute allows its students, most of whom are working, to take courses part-time and to accumulate credits in stages until successfully earning a degree. It had no campus in the beginning, and Professor Young, as pro-vice-chancellor of HKU, responded positively to the

Figure 6.1: Professor Young, one of the judges for selecting the South China Morning Post Student-of-the-Year Awards, 1990.

requests of the institute to hold classes on the HKU campus in the evenings. In 1995, the Open Learning Institute acquired university status and became the Open University of Hong Kong; in September 2021, it was renamed Hong Kong Metropolitan University.

Professor Young was also closely associated with the Caritas Institute of Higher Education since its early stages. In 1985, when the post-secondary college was established, it was called Caritas Francis Hsu College, named after Francis Hsu, the Catholic Bishop of Hong Kong from 1968 to 1973. Father Michael Ming-Cheung Yeung, who was bishop from 2014 to 2019, invited Professor Young to assist in the selection of suitable teachers for the institution, which she continues to do. In May 2011, the college was granted degree-conferring status up to the bachelor level and took its current name. The Caritas Institute of Higher Education offers courses in many disciplines and at present is responsible for training a large number of nurses in Hong Kong. Because of the shortage of nurses in long-term care services, the government offers subsidy and scholarships to mature students who enter the nursing field.[43] As with Hong Kong Metropolitan University, the Caritas Institute of Higher Education serves mainly students who are older than their counterparts at other universities, giving mature individuals a second chance at higher education.

Her Contributions to Education

Education ranks high among the priorities of Hong Kong citizens. The city's metamorphosis into a major centre for trade, finance, and communication in the 1980s was dependent not only on a stable political and economic environment but also on having a well-educated and efficient workforce.

Professor Young's appointment by the government to chair the EC was the most significant of her contributions to primary and secondary education. Since the 1980s, education policies in Hong Kong changed from increasing the number to improving the quality. She was responsible

---

43. 'Enrolled Nurse Training Programme for Welfare Sector 2023–24 Invites Applications', https://www.info.gov.hk/gia/general/202301/16/P2023011500497.htm.

for the publication of ECR-6 and ECR-7 in the 1990s. ECR-6 mainly concerns policies to improve the language abilities of the workforce and to improve the quality of teachers. ECR-7 deals with quality assurance of education by internal and external reviews using the best indicators for assessment of education and establishing school-based management. The proposals in these two reports could have far-reaching effects on the education system and society. Unfortunately, the impact of most of these policies has yet to be fully analysed. Although the themes and the ideas behind the two ECRs had been discussed in previous EC meetings, and the proposals in the two reports arose mainly from the members of the EC and not Professor Young's initiatives, it was her skill as chairman, her leadership, experience in research, wisdom, sincerity, and integrity that earned her much respect from the stakeholders represented on the EC and fostered the necessary support in the final publishing of these two important reports.

Professor Young supports institutions that provide higher education for mature students so as to enable them to upgrade their education and their jobs. She has been invited to participate in a number of scholarship and fellowship committees to select the best candidates to receive awards for advancing their studies locally or for training abroad. In this respect, she has been in the key position to select the brightest and the best young people for the future development and advancement of Hong Kong.

Conclusion

Professor Rosie Young has devoted her life selflessly to the Department of Medicine, the Faculty of Medicine, the University of Hong Kong, and to the larger community she lives in. Her contributions to the university, to medicine, and to educational policies in Hong Kong are invaluable and innumerable.

She is a tireless teacher who loves teaching and is much admired and respected by her students and colleagues. She considers the passing on of knowledge to the next generation as vital for societal progress. It is not surprising that she is recognized as one of the best teachers in the Faculty of Medicine. She taught generations of doctors who form the bulk of the medical staff in Hong Kong today.

As a pro-vice-chancellor of HKU from 1985 to 1993, and later as acting pro-vice-chancellor for another year, Professor Young served at a time when the university greatly expanded as enrolment doubled and six new faculties were added, accompanied by an extensive building programme. While she humbly denied that she had any specific contributions to the university because all major decisions were made collectively by the Senior Management Team, one can readily identify her contributions to the general well-being of staff and students from the committees that she chaired during this period. The initiative that she implemented to obtain internal university funding for research by competition and not by allocation, and her innovation to teach junior academic staff to prepare better grant applications, enhanced the competitiveness of HKU to obtain external funds for research. There is no doubt that her administrative work accorded to the advancement of academic standing and reputation of HKU and improvement of the staff-student relationship during this period.

A compassionate and highly competent physician, Professor Young benefited the thousands of patients she attended. She pioneered the Endocrinology and Metabolic Diseases Unit at Queen Mary Hospital and trained all the subspecialists in the discipline during that era. Her work as the chairman of the Medical Council of Hong Kong, the Working Party on Primary Health Care, and as a member of the Provisional Hospital Authority and Hospital Authority helped raise the professional standard of physicians and improved primary health care and hospital care for the citizens of Hong Kong. Additionally, her role in the SARS Expert Committee and in the committee to ensure the implementation of the recommendations resulted in heightening Hong Kong's preparedness in response to medical disasters. Very few physicians in the history of Hong Kong can match Professor Young in contributions to the wide spectrum of medical and health services and medical education in Hong Kong.

When serving as the chairman of the Education Commission from 1993 to 1998, Professor Young was responsible for the publication of ECR-6 and ECR-7, which could have far-reaching effects on the education system and society if implemented properly. While the quality of teachers has improved as a result of ECR-6 and the regulation that all teachers should have a university degree, whether the standards of Chinese and English among students were raised requires further evaluation. The full impact of ECR-7 dealing with quality assurance of education has yet to be fully analysed. The rapid pace of implementation and the aggressive top-down approach in the execution of these policies had led to some problems.[1] Nevertheless, it was Professor Young's leadership, her wisdom, her honesty and integrity in chairing the Education Commission that these two reports were produced.

In honour of her dedicated and sterling service in teaching, research, and administrative work, HKU conferred on her a Doctor of Science

---

1. 曾榮光,《香港教育政策分析》(香港：三聯書店香港有限公司, 2011), xiii.

degree (*honoris causa*) in 1995,[2] and emeritus professorship in 1999 on her retirement. In 2019, she further received an honorary university fellowship from HKU.[3] She was bestowed honorary degrees by the Open Learning Institute of Hong Kong, City University of Hong Kong, and Hong Kong Shue Yan University, and fellowship by the Hong Kong Academy of Medicine. Internationally, she is a fellow of the Royal Colleges of Physicians of London and Edinburgh, the Royal College of Physicians and Surgeons of Glasgow, and the Royal Australasian College of Physicians. She received honorary fellowships from the Hong Kong College of Physicians and the Hong Kong College of Family Physicians.

For her dedicated public service work, she was made an Officer of the Most Excellent Order of the British Empire (OBE) in 1987, and Commander of the Most Excellent Order of the British Empire (CBE) in 1996 by the British colonial administration. After her retirement, she received more honours for her distinguished public service: the Gold Bauhinia Star (GBS) in 2002, and the Grand Bauhinia Medal (GBM) in 2018 from the government of the Hong Kong Special Administrative Region. A complete list of her awards and honours can be found in Appendix 1.

Professor Young is a highly respected, a treasured figure and a pillar of strength in HKU and in Hong Kong community. The story of her life reveals some of the secrets of her success that one can learn and emulate. She is endowed with many talents, including intelligence, a photographic memory, courage, and an innate ability to lead. But good genes alone are not adequate, a quality nurturing environment is equally important. Professor Young has a happy childhood and loving parents who were not only affectionate but also confident of her abilities. She was also given the opportunities and encouragement from her father to choose her

---

2. 149th Congregation, 1995, Rosie Young Tse Tse, Doctor of Science (*honoris causa*), accessed 7 August 2023, https://www4.hku.hk/hongrads/citations/o-b-e-m-d-f-r-c-p-f-r-c-p-e-d-f-r-c-p-glass-f-r-a-c-p-f-h-k-a-m-medicine-j-p-rosie-tse-tse-young-rosie-young-tse-tse.

3. 2019 Honorary University Fellowship, Professor Rosie Young Tse Tse, accessed 7 August 2023, https://www4.hku.hk/honfellows/honorary-university-fellows/professor-rosie-tse-tse-young.

Figure 7.1: Professor Young awarded OBE from Governor David Wilson, 1987.

own career and he offered her appropriate guidance when necessary. In the early years of her medical career, she had excellent and understanding mentors, including Professor A. J. S. McFadzean, Professor Hou Pao Chang, Dr Gerald Chao, and Dr C. P. Fong. They taught her not only clinical skills but also the moral and ethical aspects of the profession, encouraging her to do whatever she could to help her patients.

Her capacity for hard work, her tenacity and perseverance, kindness, honesty, and integrity also ensured her success. When she encountered failure, she did her best to discern the reasons and took steps to rectify them. Other rare qualities include her willingness to admit a mistake publicly when it is called for and her perpetual optimism in life.

Professor Young is an icon and a role model for us all, especially for women. We have much to learn from her as a physician, an educator, and an administrator, as well as her attitude to life.

Appendix 1

Curriculum Vitae of Rosie Young (alias Yeung Tse Tse Rosie Margaret)

Honours

1971	Justice of the Peace in Hong Kong
1987	Officer in the Most Excellent Order of the British Empire (OBE)
1988	Honorary Fellow, Newnham College, University of Cambridge
1989	Awarded Daiichi-Mallinckrodt Prize at the 4th Asia and Oceania Thyroid Association meeting in Seoul, Korea
1995	DSc (*honoris causa*), University of Hong Kong
1995	DSc (*honoris causa*), Open Learning Institute of Hong Kong
1995	Honorary Fellow, Hong Kong College of Physicians
1995	Honorary Fellow, Hong Kong College of Family Medicine
1996	Commander in the Most Excellent Order of the British Empire (CBE)
2002	Gold Bauhinia Star, The Government of the Hong Kong Special Administrative Region (GBS)
2006	DSc (*honoris causa*), City University of Hong Kong
2013	DSocSc (*honoris causa*), Hong Kong Shue Yan University
2014	Honorary Fellow, The Provisional Hong Kong Academy of Nursing
2014	Honorary Fellow, The Hong Kong Academy of Medicine
2018	Grand Bauhinia Medal, The Government of the Hong Kong Special Administrative Region (GBM)
2019	Honorary University Fellow, The University of Hong Kong

Academic Qualifications

1953	MBBS, The University of Hong Kong
1959	MD, The University of Hong Kong

Professional Qualifications

1959	MRCP (Edinburgh)
1959	MRCP (London)
1968	FRCP (Edinburgh)
1972	FRCP (London)
1976	FRACP
1985	FRCP (Glasgow)
1989	Registered as endocrinologist with the Medical Board of Victoria, Australia
1993	Fellow of Hong Kong College of Physicians
1993	Fellow of the Hong Kong Academy of Medicine (Physician)

Current Appointments

Honorary Professor in the Department of Medicine, The University of Hong Kong
Honorary Consultant in Medicine, Queen Mary Hospital, Hong Kong
Honorary Consultant in Medicine, Hong Kong Sanatorium and Hospital

Professional Memberships

1971	American Diabetes Association
1977	Association of Physicians of Great Britain and Ireland
1977	American Endocrine Society
1982–present	Member and Deputy Chairman of the Executive Committee, The Friends of Cambridge University in Hong Kong
1983	Founding Member of the Society for the Study of Endocrinology, Metabolism and Reproduction, Hong Kong
1986	Founding Member of the Hong Kong College of Physicians
1987	Australian Endocrine Society

Appointments in the University of Hong Kong

1954–1974	Clinical Assistant, Lecturer, Senior Lecturer, and Reader in the Department of Medicine
1974–1999	Professor, Department of Medicine
1978–1983	Sub-dean (Assistant Dean), Faculty of Medicine

1983–1984	Dean, Faculty of Medicine
1985–1993	Pro-Vice-Chancellor and Senior Pro-Vice-Chancellor
1996–1997	Acting Pro-Vice-Chancellor
1997–1999	Acting Dean of Students
2000–present	Emeritus Professor
2014–present	Chairman, The University of Hong Kong Foundation for Educational Development and Research
2015–2021	Member, The Council of the University of Hong Kong

Overseas Academic Appointments

1958–1959	Sino-British Research Fellow at the Department of Medicine, University of Glasgow, UK
1963–1964	Smith and Nephew Research Fellow, Department of Biochemistry, Cambridge University, UK
1964	Welcome Research Fellow, Department of Endocrinology, Royal Postgraduate Medical School, Hammersmith Hospital, London, UK
1968 and 1970	China Medical Board Fellow, Department of Endocrinology, University of Michigan Medical School, Ann Arbor, and Metabolic Research Unit, University of California Medical Centre, San Francisco, US
1975	Visiting Fellow, Chapter of Physicians, Academy of Medicine, Singapore

Public Services and Other Appointments in Hong Kong

Medicine

1981–1988	Member, Board of Governors, Prince Philip Dental Hospital
1986–1988	Chairman, Licentiate Committee of the Medical Council of Hong Kong
1986–1988	Member, Hong Kong Government Working Party on Postgraduate Medical Education and Training
1988–1996	Chairman, The Medical Council of Hong Kong
1988–1990	Member, Provisional Hospital Authority
1989–1991	Chairman, Working Party on Primary Health Care in Hong Kong
1990–1996	Member, Hospital Authority

1992–1996	Chairman, Hospital Governing Committee, Princess Margaret Hospital
2003	Member, HKSAR Appointed SARS Expert Committee
2003	Member, HKSAR Appointed Monitoring Committee on Implementation of the SARS Expert Committee Report's Recommendations
2003–2009	Member, Research Council for Health and Health Services Research Fund and Research Fund for the Control of Infectious Diseases, Health, Welfare and Food Bureau
2006–2012	Member, Medical Assessment Board, Health, Welfare and Food Bureau, Government of the Hong Kong Special Administrative Region

Education

1987–1993	Member, The Hong Kong Examination Authority
1993–1998	Chairman, The Education Commission
1994–1996	Chairman, Language Fund Advisory Committee
1998–present	Chairman, Hong Kong Sino-British Trust Scholars' Foundation
1999–2005	Member, School Management Committee, Chinese Foundation Secondary School
2002–2003	Chairman, Second Round "Teaching and Learning Quality Process Review (TLQPR)" Panel, University Grants Committee, for tertiary institutions in Hong Kong
2003	Chairman, The Medical Council of Hong Kong "Visiting Team for the Review of Medical Education and Training in the University of Hong Kong and Chinese University of Hong Kong"
2003–present	Member, College Council and Board of Governors of the Caritas Francis Hsu College and Caritas Bianchi College of Careers (now Caritas Institute of Higher Education)
2005–present	Chairman, School Management Committee, Chinese Foundation Secondary School

Other

1986–1989	President, The Society for the Study of Endocrinology, Metabolism and Reproduction, Hong Kong
1987–1992	Council Member, The Hong Kong College of Physicians
1999– 2004	Chairman, Hong Kong University Medical Faculty Alumni
2001–2013	Chairman, Make-A-Wish Foundation of Hong Kong, Limited

Appointments in China

1998	Appointed Advisory Professor of Fudan University
2003	Appointed Member, Fudan University Council

Overseas Appointments

1974–1996	Member, Editorial Board of Medical Progress of Australian Drug Information Services
1978–1984	Secretary, National Committee of the International Research Fellowship Program, Fogarty International Center, NIH, US
1982–1999	Assessor, National Health and Medical Research Council, Commonwealth of Australia
1984–1997	Member, Editorial Board of the *Journal of the American Medical Association*, Southeast Asia Edition
1985–1997	Council Member, Asia and Oceania Thyroid Association
1984–1988	Member, Editorial Board of Diabetes Research and Clinical Practice
1987–1999	Assessor, Anti-Cancer Council of Victoria, Australia
1987–1997	Overseas Advisor, The Royal College of Physicians of Edinburgh
1988–1997	Member, Scientific Advisory Panel, Ciba Foundation, London
1989–1994	Corresponding Member, Asia Pacific Committee, RACP
1993–1996	Council Member, RACP

Appendix 2

Publications of Professor Young Tse Tse, Rosie

1. McFadzean, A.J.S., and T.T. Yeung. Hypoglycaemia in primary carcinoma of the Liver. Archives of Internal Medicine 98:720–731, 1956.
2. Watson, C.W., R. Yeung, and E.M. McGirr. Electrophoresis of thyroid proteins. Scottish Medical Journal, 5:23–29, 1960.
3. McFadzean, A.J.S., and T.T. Yeung. Hypoglycaemia in suppurative pan-cholangitis due to Clonorchis sinensis. Transactions of the Royal Society of Tropical Medicine and Hygiene, 59:179–181, 1965.
4. McFadzean, A.J.S., and T.T. Yeung. Acute pancreatitis due to Clonorchis sinensis. Transactions of the Royal Society of Tropical Medicine and Hygiene, 60:466–470, 1966.
5. McFadzean, A.J.S., and R. Yeung. Periodic paralysis complicating thyrotoxicosis in Chinese. British Medical Journal, 1:451–455, 1967.
6. McFadzean, A.J.S., and R. Yeung. Diabetes among the Chinese in Hong Kong. Diabetes, 17:219–228, 1968.
7. Lai, S.K., A.J.S. McFadzean, and R. Yeung. Microembolic pulmonary hypertension in pyogenic cholangitis. British Medical Journal, 1:22–24, 1968.
8. McFadzean, A.J.S., and R.T.T. Yeung. Further observation in hypoglycaemia in hepatocellular carcinoma. American Journal of Medicine, 47:220–235, 1969.
9. McFadzean, A.J.S., and R. Yeung. Familial occurrence of thyrotoxic periodic paralysis. British Medical Journal, 1:760, 1969.
10. Irvine, W.J., A.J.S. McFadzean, D. Todd, S.C. Tso and R.T.T. Yeung. Pernicious anaemia in the Chinese: A clinical and immunological study. Clinical and Experimental Immunology, 4:375–386, 1969.
11. Au, K.S., and R.T.T. Yeung. Thyrotoxic periodic paralysis: Periodic variation in the muscle calcium pump activity. Arch of Neurology, 26:534–546, 1972.

12. Yeung, R.T.T., D.C.Y. Yeung, and K.S. Au. Hypoglycaemia associated with lipid accumulation in primary hepatocellular carcinoma. Cancer, 32:1482–1489, 1973.
13. So, P.L., T.K. Chan, S.K. Lam, C.S. Teng, R.T.T. Yeung and D. Todd. Cortisol metabolism in glucose-6-phosphate dehydrogenase deficiency. Metabolism, 22:1443–1448, 1973.
14. Yeung, R.T.T. Effects of propranolol in plasma growth hormone response to insulin-induced hypoglycaemia in thyrotoxic patients. Journal of Clinical Endocrinology and Metabolism, 37:968–971, 1973.
15. Yeung, R.T.T., and T.F. Tse. Thyrotoxic periodic paralysis: Effect of propranolol. American Journal of Medicine, 57:584–590, 1974.
16. Yeung, R.T.T., and C.C.L. Wang. A study of carbohydrate metabolism in postnecrotic cirrhosis of liver. Gut, 15:907–912, 1974.
17. Yeung, R.T., and L.K.F. Chan. A study of diabetes mellitus among the Chinese in Hong Kong. Proceedings of the Fifth Asia and Oceania Congress of Endocrinology, Vol. II, 368–376, 1974.
18. Yeung, R.T.T. Hypoglycaemia in primary carcinoma of liver. The Bulletin of the Hong Kong Medical Association, 26:115–129, 1974.
19. Yeung, R.T.T., and L.K.F. Chan. A study of diabetes mellitus and its complications among the Chinese of Hong Kong. Philippine Journal of Internal Medicine, 13:56–61, 1975.
20. Yeung, R.T.T., and C.C.L. Wang. Disturbances of carbohydrate metabolism in cirrhosis — pseudo diabetic syndrome. Philippine Journal of Internal Medicine, 13:180–186, 1975.
21. Yeung, R.T.T., C.C.L. Wang, and L.K.F. Chan. Treatment of diabetes mellitus in Hong Kong. Philippine Journal of Internal Medicine, 13:152–156, 1975.
22. Yeung, R.T.T., C.C.L. Wang, and L.K.F. Chan. The clinical and biochemical patterns of diabetes mellitus in Hong Kong. Excerpta Medica ICS No. 390, 131–136, 1976.
23. Yeung, R.T.T. Thyroid disease in Southeast Asia. Medical Progress, 3:16–17, 1976.
24. Yeung, R.T.T. Treatment of diabetes mellitus in Southeast Asia. Medical Progress, 4:15–16, 1977.
25. Wang, C., R.T.T. Yeung, J.P. Coghlan, C.J. Oddie, B.A. Scoggins, and J.R. Stockigt. Hypertension due to 17 alpha-hydroxylase deficiency. Australian and New Zealand Journal of Medicine, 8:295–299, 1978.
26. Chan, V., C. Wang, and R.T.T. Yeung. Pituitary thyroid responses to surgical stress. Acta Endocrinologica, 88:490–498, 1978.

27. Yeung, R.T.T. Epidemiology of Diabetes in Asia and Oceania. Proceedings of 6th Asia and Oceania Congress of Endocrinology, Vol. 1, 217–226, 1978.
28. Yeung, R.T.T. Certain biochemical abnormalities in thyrotoxic periodic paralysis. Proceedings of 6th Asia and Oceania Congress of Endocrinology, Vol. 1, 300–307, 1978.
29. Wang, C., V. Chan, and R.T.T. Yeung. Effect of surgical stress on pituitary-testicular function. Clinical Endocrinology, 9:255–266, 1978.
30. Wang, C., V. Chan, T.F. Tse and R.T.T. Yeung. Effect of acute myocardial infarction on pituitary testicular function. Clinical Endocrinology, 9:249–254, 1978.
31. Wang, C., V. Chan and R.T.T. Yeung. The effect of heroin addiction on pituitary testicular function. Clinical Endocrinology, 9:455–461, 1979.
32. Chan, V., C. Wang and R.T.T. Yeung. Thyrotropin, alpha- and beta-subunits of thyrotropin and prolactin responses to 4-hour constant infusion of thyrotropin-releasing hormone in normal subjects and patients with pituitary-thyroid disorders. Journal of Clinical Endocrinology and Metabolism, 49:127–131, 1979.
33. Chan, V., C. Wang and R.T.T. Yeung. Effects of heroin addiction on thyrotropin, thyroid hormones and prolactin secretion in man. Clinical Endocrinology, 10:557–565, 1979.
34. Wang, C., V. Chan and R.T.T. Yeung. Treatment of acromegaly with Bromocriptine. Australia and New Zealand Journal of Medicine, 9:225–232, 1979.
35. Yeung, R.T.T. Diabetes Mellitus: current treatment. Medical Progress, 6:13–20, 1979.
36. Chan, V., C. Wang and R.T.T. Yeung. Dissociated thyroxine, triiodothyronine and reverse triiodothyronine levels in patients with familial goitre due to iodide organification defects. Clinical Endocrinology, 11:257–265, 1979.
37. Yeung, R.T.T. Diabetes among the Chinese in Hong Kong and Epidemiology of Diabetes in Developing Countries. edited by M.M.S. Ahuja, Interprint, pp. 21–28, 1979.
38. Teng, C.S. and R.T.T. Yeung. Changes in thyroid-stimulating antibody activity in Grave's disease treated with antithyroid drug and its relationship to relapse: a prospective study. JCEM 50:144–147, 1980.
39. Teng, C.S., R.T.T. Yeung, R.K.K. Khoo and T.T. Alagaratnam. A prospective study of the changes in thyrotrophin-binding inhibitory immunoglobulins in Grave's disease treated by subtotal thyroidectomy or radioactive iodine. Journal of Clinical Endocrinology and Metabolism, 50:1005–1010, 1980.
40. Teng, C.S., T.C. Tong, J.H. Hutchison and R.T.T. Yeung. Thyroid-stimulating immunoglobulins in neonatal Grave's disease. Archives of Diseases of Childhood, 55:894–895, 1980.

41. Chan, V., C. Wang and R.T.T. Yeung. Dissociated thyroxine, triiodothyronine and reverse triiodothyronine levels in patients with familial goitre due to iodine organification defect. Year Book of Medicine 1980, pp. 498–499, Year Book Medical Publishers, Chicago.
42. Chan, V., C. Wang, P.C. Ho, R.T.T. Yeung and H.K. Ma. Biochemical thyroid hyperfunction in trophoblastic disease. Thyroid Research VIII Proceedings of the 8th International Thyroid Congress, Sydney, Australia, 3–8 February, 1980. pp. 598–600.
43. Yeung, R.T.T., C.C.L. Wang, C.S. Teng and S.Y.L. Kwan. Extrathyroidal manifestations of hyperthyroidism. A glimpse into the eighties. Proceedings of XV Malaysian Singapore Congress of Medicine, 4–7 December 1980, Kuala Lumpur, pp. 137–139.
44. Best, J.D., V. Chan, R. Khoo, C.S. Teng, C. Wang and R.T.T. Yeung. Incidence of hypothyroidism after radioactive iodine therapy for thyrotoxicosis in Hong Kong Chinese. Clinical Radiology, 32:57–61, 1981.
45. Wang, C., T.K. Chan, R.T.T. Yeung, J.P. Coghlan, B.A. Scoggins and J.R. Stockigt. The effects of triamterene and sodium intake on renin, aldosterone and erythrocyte sodium transport in Liddle's syndrome. Journal of Clinical Endocrinology & Metabolism, 52:1027–1032, 1981.
46. Yeung, Rosie T.T., Christina Wang, C.S. Teng and Susan Kwan. The prevalence of cardiovascular complications in Chinese diabetic subjects. In: Genetic Environmental Interaction in Diabetes Mellitus, Edited by J.S. Melish, J. Hanna & S. Baba, Excerpta Medica, ICS 549, pp. 277–281, 1981.
47. Kawa, A., Y. Kono, Y. Hamasaki, T. Kayumi, S. Sakaguchi, S. Nakamura, N. Arima, N. Koreeda, K. Nomoto, V. Skultab, R.E. Fernando, F.M. Pascasio, R.T.T. Yeung and C.S. Teng. Possible racial variations in HLA-diabetes association in Japanese and Southeast Asian populations. In: Genetic Environmental Interaction in Diabetes Mellitus. Edited by J.S. Melish, J. Hanna, S. Baba, Excerpta Medica, ICS 549, pp. 141–147, 1981.
48. Teng, C.S., R.T.T. Yeung, A. Kawa, S. Nakamura, K. Nomoto, N. Arima, N. Koreeda, K. Tsuji and P.W.M. Ho. Thyrotrophin-binding inhibitory immunoglobulins and HLA-DRW 3 – Two prognostic factors in Graves' Disease. Australian and New Zealand Journal of Medicine, Vol. 11, pp. 383–385, 1981.
49. S.Y. Cheung, Rosie T.T. Young and G.B. Ong. Surgery of the adrenal gland – a review of 42 cases. Southeast Asian Journal of Surgery, Vol. 4, No. 2, pp. 9–19, July 1981.
50. T.K. Chan, Vivian N.Y. Chan, C.S. Teng and R.T.T. Yeung. Effects du gliclazide et du glibenclamide sur les fonctions plaquettaires, la fibrinolyse et l'équilibre

glycemique chez des diabetiques presentant une retinopathie. Semaine des Hopitaux de Paris, Vol. 58, No. 19, pp. 1197–1200, May 1982.

51. C.S. Teng, Patricia Ho and <u>Rose T.T. Yeung</u>. Down-regulation of insulin receptors in post-necrotic cirrhosis of the liver. Journal of Clinical Endocrinology and Metabolism, Vol. 55, No. 3, pp. 524–533, September 1982.

52. Joana C.I. Ai Ho, <u>Rose T.T. Yeung</u> and K.C. Lam. Spontaneous regression of hepatocellular carcinoma – a case study. Cancer, Vol. 50, No. 2, pp. 332–336, July 1982.

53. B.M. Jones, C.S. Teng and <u>Rose T.T. Yeung</u>. Evaluation of T cell, T-helper cell, and T-suppressor-cell function in patients with Graves' disease before and after treatment with anti-thyroid drugs. Clinical Immunology and Immunopathology, Vol. 25, No. 2, pp. 232–242, November 1982.

54. <u>Yeung, Rose T.T.</u> Diabetes in S.E. Asia, viewpoint from Hong Kong. Medical Progress, 15–16, Vol. 9, No. 6, 1982.

55. <u>Rose T.T. Yeung</u>. Patient management in endocrine disease. Medical Progress, pp. 44–45, 1982.

56. <u>R.T.T. Yeung</u>, A. Kawa, K. Kono, K. Nanjo, R.E. Fernando and E. Aiyathurai. HLA-diabetes association among Southeast Asian populations. In: Clinico-Genetic Genesis of Diabetes Mellitus. Excerpta Medica ICS 597, pp. 105–113, 1982.

57. <u>R.T.T. Yeung</u>, D.C.Y. Yeung and S.S.C. Wong. Hypoglycaemia in primary hepatoma. In: Insulin-Like Growth Factors/Somatomedins, published by Walter de Guyter & Co., pp. 325–328, 1983.

58. <u>Rose T.T. Yeung</u>, Christina C.L. Wang and Karen S.L. Lam. Common Metabolic and Endocrinological Disorders in Southeast Asia. Medical Progress Special Issue, pp. 51–57, 1983.

59. K.K. Pun, C.K. Yeung, P.W.M. Ho, H.J. Lin, M.K. Chan and <u>R.T.T. Yeung</u>. Effects of propranolol and hemodialysis on the response of glucose, insulin, C-peptide and cyclic AMP to glucagon challenge. Clinical Nephrology, Vol. 21, No. 4, (April) 1984. pp. 235–240.

60. T.K. Chan, V. Chan, C.S. Teng and <u>R.T.T. Yeung</u>. Effects du gliclazide et du glibenclamide sur les fonctions plaquettaires, la fibrinolyse et l'equilibre glycemique chez les diabetiques presentant une retinopathie. Le Journal International de Medicine, Vol. 9, No. 51, pp. 67–70, 1984.

61. T.F. Fok, V. Chan, F.T. Lee, K.H. Chan, <u>R.T.T. Yeung</u> and J.H. Hutchison. Neonatal screening for congenital hypothyroidism in Hong Kong Chinese. Asean Journal of Clinical Sciences, Vol. 4, pp. 179–182, 1983.

62. E.A. Benson, P. Ho, C. Wang, P.C. Wu, P.N. Fredland and R.T.T. Yeung. Insulin Autoimmunity as a Cause of Hypoglycaemia. Archives of Internal Medicine, Vol. 144, pp. 2351–2354, 1984.

63. J.T.C. Ma, C. Wang, F.C.S. Ho, K.S.L. Lam, R.T.T. Yeung. Primary hypothyroidism and essential hypernatraemia in a patient with histiocytosis X. Australian New Zealand Journal of Medicine, Vol. 15, pp. 72–74, 1985.

64. K.K. Pun, C.K. Yeung and R.T.T. Yeung. Effects of Propranolol and Metoprolol on Glucose Cyclic AMP and Insulin Responses during Pharmacological Hypergluconaemia in Haemodialysis Patients. Nephron, Vol. 39, pp. 175–178, 1985.

65. Rose T.T. Yeung. The Development of Medical Education in Hong Kong. Chronicle. Royal College of Physicians of Edinburgh, Vol. 15, No. 3, pp. 188–196, July 1985.

66. B.R. Hawkins, J.T.C. Ma, K.S.L. Lam, C.C.L. Wang and R.T.T. Yeung. Analysis of linkage between HLA haplotype and susceptibility to Graves' disease in multiple-case Chinese families in Hong Kong. Acta Endocrinologica, Vol. 110, pp. 66–69, 1985.

67. B.R. Hawkins, J.T.C. Ma, K.S.L. Lam, C.C.L. Wang and R.T.T. Yeung. Association of HLA Antigens with Thyrotoxic Graves' Disease and periodic paralysis in Hong Kong Chinese. Clinical Endocrinology, Vol. 23, pp. 245–252, 1985.

68. C. Wang and R.T.T. Yeung. Gossypol and hypokalaemia. Contraception, 32:237–253, 1985.

69. B.R. Hawkins, M.S.M. Ip, K.S.L. Lam, J.T.C. Ma, W.Y. Chan-Lui, R.T.T. Yeung, and R.L. Dawkins. HLA Antigens and acetylcholine receptor antibody in the subclassification of myasthenia gravis in Hong Kong Chinese. Journal of Neurology, Neurosurgery and Psychiatry, Vol. 49, pp. 316–320, 1986.

70. K.K. Pun, P.W.M. Ho and R.T.T. Yeung. Anomalous Cyclic 3'5'-monophosphate response to glucagon in patients with hepatocellular carcinoma. Cancer Research 46:2152–2154, 1986.

71. K.K. Pun, C.K. Yeung and R.T.T. Young. Propranolol-induced Hypoglycaemia in a hemodialysis patient. Dialysis and Transplantation, 15:195–196, 1986.

72. K.S.L. Lam, C.Wang, J.T.C. Ma, S.P. Leung, R.T.T. Yeung. Hypothalamic defects in 2 adult patients with septo-optic dysplasia. Acta Endocrinologica, 112:305–309, 1986.

73. J.T.C. Ma, C. Wang, K.S.L. Lam, R.T.T. Yeung, F.L. Chan, J. Boey, P.S.Y. Cheung, J.P. Coghlan, B.A. Scoggins, H.J.R. Stockigt. A study of 50 consecutive patients with hyperaldosteronism in Hong Kong Chinese. Quarterly Journal of Medicine, 61:1021–1037, 1986.

74. K.S.L. Lam, C. Wang, R.T.T. Yeung, J.T.C. Ma, J.H.C. Ho, V.K.C. Tse, N. Ling. Hypothalamic hypopituitarism following cranial irradiation for nasopharyngeal carcinoma. Clinical Endocrinology, 24:643–651, 1986.
75. Karen S.L. Lam, Rose T.T. Yeung and M.K. Chan. High-density lipoprotein cholesterol, hepatic lipase and lipoprotein lipase activities in thyroid dysfunction – effects of treatment. Quarterly Journal of Medicine, 59(229):513–521, 1986.
76. Karen S.L. Lam, John T.C. Ma, Edith Y.M. Chan & Rose T.T. Yeung. Sustained improvement in diabetic control in long-term self-monitoring of blood glucose. Diabetes Research and Clinical Practice, 2:165–171, 1986.
77. R.T.T. Yeung, K.S.L. Lam, & J.T.C. Ma. Problems in the treatment of diabetes in Hong Kong. In: World Book of Diabetes in Practice. Edited by Leo Krall, Vol. 2, 236–238, 1986.
78. K.K. Pun, C.K. Yeung, W. Chak, P.W.M. Ho, M.K. Chan, H.L. Lin & R.T.T. Yeung. Effects of selective and non-selective Beta Blockers on the alanine & free fatty acid responses to glucagon challenge in haemodialysis patients. Clinical Nephrology, 26:222–226, 1986.
79. Karen S.L. Lam, Rose T.T. Yeung, Patricia W.M. Ho & S.K. Lam. Glucose intolerance in thyrotoxicosis – Roles of insulin glucagon & somatostalin. Acta Endocrinologica, Vol. 114, 228–234, 1987.
80. R.T.T. Yeung and Karen S.L. Lam. Thyroid Disorders in the Far East in the Chapter "Endocrine Disorders", Oxford Textbook of Medicine, edited by D.J. Weatherall, J.G.G. Ledingham and D.A. Warrell, Oxford Medical Publications, 10.48–10.50, 1987.
81. Karen S.L. Lam, Vincent K.C. Tse, Christina Wang, Rosie T.T. Yeung, John T.C. Ma and J.H.C. Ho. Early effects of cranial irradiation on hypothalamic-pituitary function. Journal of Clinical Endocrinology and Metabolism, 64:418–424, 1987.
82. John T.C. Ma and John H.C. Ho. Early effects of cranial irradiation of hypothalamic pituitary function. Journal of Clinical Endocrinology and Metabolism, Vol. 64, 418–424, 1987.
83. Annie W.C. Kung, John T.C. Ma, Christina Wang, K.H. Fu, Karen S.L. Lam, Rosie T.T. Yeung and J. Boey. Prevention of hypoglycaemia in a patient with pancreatic microadenomatosis by a long-acting somatostatin analogue SMS 201–995. Clinical Endorcinology 27:469–473, 1987.
84. S.L. Lam, Rose T.T. Yeung, John Boey. Prevention of Hypoglycaemia in a patient with Pancreatic microadenomatosis by a long-acting somatostatin analogue SMS 201–995. Clinical Endocrinology 27, 469–473, 1987.

85. A.W.C. Kung, J.T.C. Ma, Y.L. Yu, C. Wang, E.K.W. Woo, K.S.L. Lam, <u>R.T.T. Yeung</u>. Myopathy in acute hypothyroidism. Postgraduate Medical Journal, 63, 661–663, 1987.
86. K.S.L. Lam, J.H.C. Ho, A.W.M. Lee, V.K.C. Tse, P.K. Chan, C. Wang, J.T.C. Ma and <u>R.T.T. Yeung</u>. Symptomatic hypothalamic-pituitary dysfunction in nasopharyngeal carcinoma – a retrospective study. International Journal of Radiation Oncology, Biology & Physics 13, 1343–1350, 1987.
87. B.R. Hawkins, K.S.L. Lam, J.T.C. Ma, C. Wang and <u>R.T.T. Yeung</u>. Strong association between HLA-DRW9 and Hashimoto's Thyroiditis in Southern Chinese. Acta Endocrinology, 114, 543–546, 1987.
88. C. Wang, K.S.L. Lam, J. Ma, T. Chan, M.Y. Lui & <u>R.T.T. Yeung</u>. Long term treatment of hyperprolactinaemia with bromocriptine: effect of drug withdrawal. Clinical Endocrinology 27, 363–371, 1987.
89. A.W.C. Kung, John T.C. Ma, Vivian Wong, Christina Wang, Karen S.L. Lam, <u>R.T.T. Yeung</u> and H.K. Ma. Glucose and lipid metabolism with low dose sequential oral contraceptives in women with history of gestational diabetes. Contraception 35, 257–269, 1987.
90. B.R. Hawkins, K.S.L. Lam, J.T.C, Ma, L.C.K. Low, P.T. Cheung, S.W. Serjeanbon & <u>R.T.T. Yeung</u>. Strong association of HLA DR3/DRW9 heterozygosity with insulin dependent diabetes mellitus of early onset in Chinese. Diabetes 36, 1297–1300, 1987.
91. K.K. Pun & <u>R.T.T. Yeung</u>. Editorial: Osteoporosis – The Silent Epidemic. JAMA 1987, 5–6.
92. P.S.Y. Cheung, J.H. Boey, C.C.L. Wang, J.T.C. Ma, K.S.L. Lam & <u>R.T.T. Yeung</u>. Primary hyperparathyroidism – its clinical pattern and results of surgical treatment in Hong Kong Chinese. Surgery 103(5):558–562, 1988.
93. K.K. Pun, P.W.H. Ho and <u>R.T.T. Yeung</u>. C-peptide in non-alcoholic cirrhosis and hepatocellular carcinoma. Journal of Endocrinological Investigation. 11:337–343, 1988.
94. K.K. Pun, <u>R.T.T. Yeung</u>, C.F. Tam & P.W.M. Ho. The use of glucagon challenge tests in the diagnostic evaluation of hypoglycaemia due to hepatoma, insulinoma and uraemia. Journal of Clinical Endocrinology and Metabolism 67:546–550, 1988.
95. L.C.K. Low, C. Wang, P.T. Cheung, P. Ho, K.S.L. Lam, <u>R.T.T. Yeung</u>, C.Y. Yeung & N. Ling. Long term pulsatile growth hormone (GH) releasing hormone therapy in children with GH deficiency. Journal of Clinical Endocrinology and Metabolism 66:611–617, 1988.

96. E. Woo, K. Lam, Y.L. Yu, J. Ma, C. Wang & R.T.T. Yeung. Temporal lobe and hypothalamic-pituitary dysfunction after radiotherapy for nasopharyngeal carcinoma – a distinct clinical syndrome. Journal of Neurology, Neurosurgery and Psychiatry 51:1302–1307, 1988.

97. Young R.T.T. To set priorities within a limited research budget – what can we do for our countries – pp. 121–127. Fourteen Congress of the Universities of the Commonwealth, Perth, February 1988.

98. K.S.L. Lam, R.T.T. Yeung, E. Benson & C. Wang. Erythrocyte Sodium-potassium pump in thyrotoxic periodic paralysis. Australian and New Zealand Journal of Medicine 19:6–10, 1989.

99. K.S.L. Lam, C. Wang, P. Choi, J. Ma & R.T.T. Yeung. Long term effect of megavoltage radiotherapy in acromegaly. Australian and New Zealand Journal of Medicine 19:202–206, 1989.

100. Pun K.K., Chan G., Wang C. & R.T.T. Yeung. Cranial diabetes insipidus presenting as pyrexia of undetermined origin. American Journal of Medicine 86:732–733, 1989.

101. J. Ma, K.S.L. Lam & R.T.T. Yeung. Diabetes in perspective. Medical Progress 16:5–7, 1989.

102. R.T.T. Yeung. Thyrotoxic Periodic Paralysis – Revisited, in Progress in Thyroidology 1989, M. Lee, C-S. Koh, C.J. Eastman, S. Nagataki (eds), Korea Medical Publishing Company, Seoul, Korea, pp. 9–12, 1989.

103. L.C.K. Low, E.C.L. Yu, O.K.W. Chow, C.Y. Yeung & R.T.T. Yeung. Hyperinsulinism in Infancy. Australian Paediatric Journal, 25:174–177, 1989.

104. Annie W.C. Kung, John T.C. Ma, Christina Wang and Rosie T.T. Yeung. Hyperthyroidism during pregnancy due to coexistence of struma ovarii and Graves' Disease. Postgraduate Medical Journal 66:132–133, 1990.

105. A.W.C. Kung, P. Choi, K.S.L. Lam, K.K. Pun, C. Wang & R.T.T. Yeung. Discriminating factors affecting early outcome of radioiodine treatment for Graves' Disease. Clinical Radiology, 42:52–54, 1990.

106. A.W.C. Kung, K.S.L. Lam, K.K. Pun, C. Wang & R.T.T. Yeung. Circulating somatostatin after oral glucose in hypothyroidism. Journal of Endocrinological Investigation, 13:403–406, 1990.

107. A.W.C. Kung, K.K. Pun, K.S.L. Lam, P. Choi, C. Wang & R.T.T. Yeung. Long term results following I131 Rx for Grave disease – discriminant factors affecting hypothyroidism. Quarterly Journal of Medicine 281:961–967, 1990.

108. A.W.C. Kung & R.T.T. Young. Autoimmunity and Endocrine Disease. JAMA (SEA edition). Vol. 5, No. 4:5–6, 1989.

109. K.K. Pun, F.H.W., C. Wang, P. Lau, P.W.M. Ho, W.K. Pun, S.P. Chow, C.L. Cheng, J.C.Y. Leong & <u>R.T.T. Yeung</u>. Vitamin D status among patients with fractured neck of femur in Hong Kong. Bone 1990, 11, 365–368.

110. <u>Rosie T.T. Young</u>. Management of Thyrotoxicosis. Medical Progress 1990, 41–50.

111. K.S.L. Lam, V.K.C. Tse, C. Wang, <u>R.T.T. Yeung</u> & H.C. Ho. Effects of cranial irradiation on hypothalamic pituitary function, a 5-year longitudinal study in patients with NPC. Quarterly Journal of Medicine 286:165–176, 1991.

112. P.C. Fong, K.K. Pun, Y.T. Tai, C. Wang and <u>Rosie T.T. Young</u>. Propylthiouracil Hypersensitivity with Circumstantial Evidence for Drug-Induced Reversible Sensorineural Deafness: A Case report. Hormone research 1991, 35:132–136.

113. A.W.C. Kung, K.K. Pun, K.S.L. Lam and <u>Rosie T.T. Yeung</u>. Rhabdomyolysis Associated with Cranial Diabetes Insipidus. Postgraduate Medical Journal 1991, 67:912–913.

114. Karen S.L. Lam, Annie W.C. Kung and <u>Rosie T.T. Young</u>. Post-irradiation Hypopituitarism Presenting as Severe Hyponatraemia. American Journal of Medicine 1992, 92, 9:219–221.

115. Y.J. Lim, E. Kwan, P.T. Cheung, K. Lam, A. Kung, C. Wang, <u>R.T.T. Young</u> and L.C.K. Low. Growth hormone deficiency in childhood: the Queen Mary Hospital experience (1978–92). Journal of Hong Kong Medical Association 1993, 45:272–277.

116. <u>R.T.T. Young</u> and K.C.B. Tan. Future Prospects in Diabetes Management. Medical Progress 1994, pp. 15–16.

117. <u>R.T.T. Yeung</u> & K.S.L. Lam. Common endocrine and metabolic disorders among the Chinese. Chinese Medical Journal 1997, Vol. 110, No. 6:425–430.

Bibliography

Archives

Colonial papers: CO 129, CO 1030.
MacDonnell to Earl of Kimberley, Chinese Hospital, 19 February 1872, CO 129/156 #947, 339.

Hong Kong Government Reports Online

Hong Kong Hansard, 1995.
Hong Kong Sessional Papers, 1896.
Hong Kong Blue Book, Section on Education, 1888, 1889.

Government Reports

Government Information Report. 'Hong Kong Population: Characteristics and Trends'. https://www.info.gov.hk/info/population/eng/pdf/report_eng.pdf.
Hong Kong Annual Digest of Statistics, 1991–2012.
Hong Kong Annual Reports, 1950–1980.
Hong Kong Medical and Health Department Annual Reports, 1961–1971.
Medical and Sanitary Report for the Year 1921, Hong Kong Administrative Report 1921.
Medical and Sanitary Report for the Year 1929, Hong Kong Administrative Report 1929.

Special Government Reports

Chung, Sir S. Y. *Report of the Provisional Hospital Authority*. Hong Kong Government. December 1989.

Colonial Secretariat. *Report on Women's Salary Scales in Public Service*. Hong Kong Government: Government Printer, 1962.

Education Commission Report No. 2. Education Bureau, Hong Kong Government. https://www.e-c.edu.hk/doc/en/publications_and_related_documents/education_reports/ecr2_e.pdf.

Education Commission Report No. 3. Education Bureau, Hong Kong Government. https://www.e-c.edu.hk/doc/en/publications_and_related_documents/education_reports/ecr3_e.pdf.

Education Commission Report No. 4. Education Bureau, Hong Kong Government. https://www.e-c.edu.hk/doc/en/publications_and_related_documents/education_reports/ecr4_e.pdf.

Education Commission Report No. 5. Education Bureau, Hong Kong Government, 1992. https://www.e-c.edu.hk/doc/en/publications_and_related_documents/education_reports/ecr5_e.pdf.

Education Commission Report No. 6, Enhancing Language Proficiency: A Comprehensive Strategy, March 1996. Education Bureau, Hong Kong Government. https://www.e-c.edu.hk/doc/en/publications_and_related_documents/education_reports/ecr6_e.pdf.

Education Commission Report No. 7. Quality of Education. September 1997. Education Bureau, The Government of HKSAR. https://www.e-c.edu.hk/doc/en/publications_and_related_documents/education_reports/ecr7_e_2.pdf.

Halnan, K. E. *Report of the Hong Kong Government Working Party on Postgraduate Medical Education and Training*. Hong Kong: Hong Kong Government Printer, October 1988.

Health for All. The Way Ahead. Report of the Working Party on Primary Care in Hong Kong. December 1990.

Hong Kong Government. *Development of Medical Services in Hong Kong*. Hong Kong: Government Printers, 1964.

Hong Kong Government. *Report of Advisory Committee on Clinics*, 1966.

Hong Kong Government. *Report of the Working Party on Unregistrable Doctors*. Colonial Secretariat, Hong Kong, 11 April 1975. https://www.edb.gov.hk/attachment/en/about-edb/publications-stat/major-reports/ecr6_e_2.pdf.

Hong Kong Government. White Paper. *Secondary Education in Hong Kong Over the Next Decade*. Tabled in the Legislative Council, 16 October 1975. https://www.eduhk.hk/cird/publications/edpolicy/02.pdf.

Hong Kong Government. *The Development of Senior Secondary and Tertiary Education in Hong Kong*, October 1978. https://www.eduhk.hk/cird/publications/edpolicy/04.pdf.

Oswald Chadwick's Report on the Sanitary Condition of Hong Kong with Appendices and Plans. Eastern No. 38. Printed for the use of the Colonial Office. November 1882, CO 882.

SARS Expert Committee Report, 2003. https://www.sars-expertcom.gov.hk/english/reports/reports.html.

Scott, W. D. *The Delivery of Medical Service in Hospitals: A Report for the Hong Kong Government*, 1985.

Selwyn-Clarke, P. S. *Report on Medical and Health Conditions in Hong Kong for the Period 1 January 1941 to 31 August 1945*, 8–10. London: His Majesty's Stationery Office, 1946.

Newspapers

Hong Kong News, February 1942–December 1944.
South China Morning Post, 1927–1933; 1945; 1957–2021.

Books

《醫路——生命是美。醫院管理局二十年》。香港：香港知出版社，2012。
曾榮光，《香港教育政策分析》。香港：三聯書店（香港）有限公司，2011。

Bergère, Marie-Claire. *Sun Yat-Sen*. Translated by Janet Lloyd. Stanford, CA: Stanford University Press, 1994.

Bolton, Kingsley. 'Hong Kong English: Autonomy and Creativity'. In *Hong Kong English: Autonomy and Creativity*, edited by Kingsley Bolton. Hong Kong: Hong Kong University Press, 2002.

Caldwell, Brian. *School-Based Management*. Educational Policy Series, International Academy of Learning and International Institute of Educational Planning, 2005. UNESCO Digital Library. https://unesdoc.unesco.org/ark:/48223/pf0000141025.

Cameron, Meribeth E. *The Reform Movement in China 1899–1912*. Stanford, CA: Stanford University Press, 1931.

Carroll, John M. *A Concise History of Hong Kong*. Lanham, MD: Rowman and Littlefield, 2007.

Chan, Jenny, and Derek Pua. *Three Years Eight Months: The Forgotten Struggle of Hong Kong's WWII*. San Francisco, CA: Pacific Atrocities Education, 2017.

Chan, Sui-jeung. *East River Column: Hong Kong Guerillas in the Second World War and After*. Hong Kong: Hong Kong University Press, 2009.

Chan Lau, Kit-Ching, and Peter Cunich. *The Impossible Dream: Hong Kong University from Foundation to Re-Establishment 1910 to 1950*. Hong Kong: Oxford University Press, 2002.

Chan-Yeung, Moira M. W. *A Medical History of Hong Kong, 1842–1941*. Hong Kong: Chinese University of Hong Kong Press, 2018.

Chan-Yeung, Moira. *A Medical History of Hong Kong, 1942–2015*. Hong Kong: Chinese University of Hong Kong Press, 2019.

Chan-Yeung, Moira. *A Medical History of Hong Kong: The Development and Contributions of Outpatient Services*. Hong Kong: Chinese University of Hong Kong Press, 2021.

Chan-Yeung, Moira M. W., and Contributors. *Daily Giving Service: A History of Diocesan Girls' School, Hong Kong*. Hong Kong: Hong Kong University Press, 2022.

Chen, Ping. 'Language Policy in Hong Kong during the Colonial Period before July 1 1997'. In *Language Planning and Language Policy: East Asian Perspectives*, edited by Ping Chen and Nanette Gottlieb, 111–28. Cornwall, UK: Curzon Press, 2001.

Cheng, Yin Cheong, and Wai Ming Cheung. 'Analysing Hong Kong Educational Policy: Application of a Comprehensive Framework'. In *Handbook in Educational Policy in Hong Kong (1965–1998)*. Hong Kong: Hong Kong Institute of Education, 1998.

Ching, Frank. *130 Years of Medicine in Hong Kong: From the College of Medicine for Chinese to Li Ka Shing Faculty of Medicine*. Singapore: Springer Nature, 2018.

Chiu, Patricia P. K. *A History of the Grant Schools Council: Mission, Vision, and Transformation*. Hong Kong: Grant Schools Council, 2013.

Cunich, Peter. *A History of the University of Hong Kong: Volume 1, 1911–1945*. Hong Kong: Hong Kong University Press, 2012.

Department of Medicine, The University of Hong Kong. *Achievements in Medicine, 1985–1995*. Hong Kong: The University of Hong Kong, 1995.

Department of Medicine (1993–2019): Impact, Inspirations. Hong Kong: The University of Hong Kong, 2021.

Endacott, G. B. *Hong Kong Eclipse*. Hong Kong: Oxford University Press, 1978.

Evans, Dafydd Emrys. *Constancy of Purpose: An Account of the Foundation and History of the Hong Kong College of Medicine and the Faculty of Medicine of the University of Hong Kong, 1887–1987*. Hong Kong: Hong Kong University Press, 1987.

Gauld, R., and D. Gould. *The Hong Kong Health Sector*. Hong Kong: Chinese University of Hong Kong Press, 2002.

Gould, Stacey Belcher, and Tina Yee-wang Pang. *HKU Memories from the Archives*. Hong Kong: HKU Museum and Art Gallery, 2013.

Han, Suyin. *My House Has Two Doors*. New York: Putnam, 1980.

Hong Kong Academy of Medicine. *Centenary Tribute to Professor AJS McFadzean: A Legacy for Medicine in Hong Kong*. Hong Kong: Hong Kong Academy of Medicine Press, 2015.

Hong Kong Academy of Medicine. *In Pursuit of Excellence: The First 10 Years, 1993–2003*. Hong Kong: Hong Kong Academy of Medicine Press, 2003.

Hong Kong Museum of Medical Science Society. *Plague, SARS, and the Story of Medicine in Hong Kong*. Hong Kong: Hong Kong University Press, 2006.

Huang, Rayson. *A Lifetime in Academia: An Autobiography*. Hong Kong: Hong Kong University Press, 2000.

Hutcheon, Robin. *Bedside Manners: Hospital and Health Care in Hong Kong*. Hong Kong: Chinese University of Hong Kong Press, 1999.

Hutcheon, Robin. *Highrise Society: The First Ten Years of Hong Kong Housing Society*. Hong Kong: Chinese University of Hong Kong Press, 1998.

Lee, Guan-kin. 'Wang Gungwu: An Oral History'. In *Power and Identity in the Chinese World Order Festschrift in Honour of Professor Wang Gungwu*, edited by Billy So, John Fitzgerald, Jian Li Huang, and James K. Chin, 375–405. Hong Kong: Hong Kong University Press, 2003.

Leung, Gabriel M., and John Bacon-Shone. *Hong Kong's Health System: Reflections, Perspectives and Visions*. Hong Kong: Hong Kong University Press, 2006.

Mak, Grace C. L. 'Women and Education'. In *Women and Girls in Hong Kong: Current Situation and Future Challenges*, edited by Susanne Y. P. Choi and Fanny M. Cheung. Hong Kong: Hong Kong Institute of Asia-Pacific Studies, the Chinese University of Hong Kong, 2012.

Mellor, Bernard. *The University of Hong Kong: An Informal History*. Hong Kong: Hong Kong University Press, 1981.

Morris, Paul, and Bob Adamson. *Curriculum, Schooling and Society in Hong Kong*, 31–33. Hong Kong: Hong Kong University Press, 2010.

Pang, Nicholas Sun-Keung. 'The Quality Assurance Movement: Lessons from Hong Kong Schools'. In *New Challenges in Education: Lessons from Around the World*, vol. 19, 83–90. Sofia: Bulgarian Comparative Education Society Conference Books, 2021.

Rhoads, Edward J. M. *China's Republican Revolution: The Case of Kwangtung, 1895–1913*. Cambridge, MA: Harvard University Press, 1975.

Sinn, Elizabeth. *Power and Charity: A Chinese Merchant Elite in Colonial Hong Kong*. Hong Kong: Hong Kong University Press, 2003.

Slavick, Madeline, and Anna Koor, eds. *Confessions and Professions: Grand Rounds in Hong Kong Medicine*. Hong Kong: MCCM Creations, 2019.

Smith, Carl T. *A Sense of History: Studies of the Social and Urban History of Hong Kong*. Hong Kong: Hong Kong Educational Publishing Co., 1995.

Starling, Arthur E. *The Chance of a Lifetime: The Birth of a New Medical School in Hong Kong*. Hong Kong: Chinese University of Hong Kong Press, 1988.

Sweeting, Anthony. *Educational History of Hong Kong, 1941 to 2001: Visions and Revisions*. Hong Kong: Hong Kong University Press, 2004.

The University of Hong Kong Li Ka Shing Faculty of Medicine. *Shaping the Health of Hong Kong: 120 Years of Achievement*, edited by Chak-sing Lau, Daniel Tak-mao

Chan, John Malcolm Nicholls, Nivritti Gajanan Patil, and Mai-har Sham. Hong Kong: Hong Kong University Press, 2006.
Tsang, Steve. *A Modern History of Hong Kong*. Hong Kong: Hong Kong University Press, 2004.
Tsin, Michael. *Nation, Governance, and Modernity in China*. Stanford, CA: Stanford University Press, 1999.
Young, Ernest. *The Presidency of Yuan Shikai: Liberalism and Dictatorship in Early Republican China*. Ann Arbor: The University of Michigan Press, 1977.

Journals

Boyle, Joseph. 'English in Hong Kong'. *English Today* 13, no. 2 (1997): 3–6.
Boyle, Joseph. 'Hong Kong's Educational System: English or Chinese?'. *Language, Culture and Curriculum* 8, no. 3 (1995): 291–302.
Cheng, Yin Cheong. 'Hong Kong Educational Reforms in the Last Decade: Reform Syndrome and New Developments'. *International Journal of Educational Management* 23, no. 1 (2009): 65–86.
Fan, Ka-wai. 'Pao-chang Hou (1893–1967): Pathologist and Historian of Chinese Medicine'. *Journal of Medical Biography* 14, no. 4 (2006): 209.
Fung, Yee Wang. 'An Analysis and Evaluation of the Precious Blood Golden Jubilee Girls' School Incident'. *Ming Pao Monthly*, July 1978, 93–97.
'Hong Kong Tops World Ranking of Dental Schools'. *Hong Kong Economic Journal*, 22 March 2016.
McFadzean, A. J. S., and T. T. Yeung. 'Hypoglycaemia in Suppurative Pancholangitis due to *Clonorchis sinensis*'. *Transactions of the Royal Society of Tropical Medicine and Hygiene* 59 (1965): 179–81.
McFadzean, A. J. S., and T. T. Yeung. 'Periodic Paralysis Complicating Thyrotoxicosis in Chinese'. *British Medical Journal* 1 (1967): 451–55.
'Obituary. A. J. S. McFadzean, OBE, DSc, MD, FRCP, FRCP Ed, FACP'. *British Medical Journal* 6 (1974): 723.
Pang, F. C., and S. S. Lai. 'Establishment of the Primary Healthcare Commission'. *Hong Kong Medical Journal* 29 (2023): 6–7.
'Professor Young Tse Tse, Rosie, Dean of Faculty of Medicine'. *Caduceus* 15, no. 4 (1983): 137–38.
Ride, Lindsay. 'Medical Education in Hong Kong'. *Caduceus* 15, no. 4 (1936): 159–71.
'Sir Ride, Lindsay C.B.E., Ed., M.A., D.M.'. *British Medical Journal* 2, no. 6096 (1977): 1228.
'Teachers Protest Following Stress-Related Suicides'. *Education International*, 23 January 2006. https://www.ei-ie.org/en/detail/54/hong-kong-teachers-protest-following-stress-related-suicides.

Yeung, R. T. T., and L. K. F. Chan, 'A Study of Diabetes Mellitus and Its Complications among the Chinese of Hong Kong'. *Philippine Journal of Internal Medicine* 13 (1975): 56–61.

Yeung, R. T. T., and T. F. Tse. 'Thyrotoxic Periodic Paralysis: Effect of Propranolol'. *American Journal of Medicine* 57 (1974): 584–90.

Yu, Y. L. Abridged version of the talk given by Prof. Sir David Todd at the Inauguration of the Medical History Interest Group Held at the Hong Kong Museum of Medical Sciences on 17 January 2009. 'Reminiscences of Three Former Teachers: Prof AJS McFadzean, Dr Stephen Chang and Prof Gerald Choa'. *Hong Kong Medical Journal* 15, no. 4 (2009): 315–19.

Zeng, Wei. 'Medium of Instruction in Secondary Education in Post-colonial Hong Kong: Why Chinese? Why English?' *Working Papers in Educational Linguistics* 22, no. 1 (2007): 42–56.

Index

Page numbers in *italics* refer to figures.

Acting Dean of Students, x, 88, 145
Acting Pro-Vice-Chancellor, ix, 88, 91, 138, 145

Banfill, Stanley Martin, 32, 34, 35
British Army Aid Group (BAAG), 33

Cambridge University, 55, 135, 144–45
Carcinoma of the Liver (hepatocellular carcinoma), 37, 56, 70
Caritas Institute of Higher Learning, 69
Centre for Health Protection, 113–14
Chan, Man-mun, Johannes, 88
Chancellor of HKU, 89–90
Chang, Stephen, 42, 43
Cheeloo University, 24, 42
Cheng, Kai Ming, 123
Cheng, Yu Tung, 79
Chief Executive of Hong Kong, 89–90, 103, 107, 115
China Medical Board (CMB), 15, 78–79
China Medical Board Fellowship, 57–58
Chinese Communist Party (CCP), 17, 19, 30, 130
Chinese Foundation Secondary School, 69, 135, 146
Chinese Language Committee, 125
Ching, Sansan, 123
Choa, Gerald, 42, *43*, 50, 80, 142
Chung Chi College, 125
Chung, S. Y., 109, *111*, 112

Commander of the Most Excellent Order of the British Empire (CBE), 140, 143
Conn, J. W., 58
COVID-19, vi, 115

Dean of the Faculty of Medicine, ix, xiii, 44, 62, 66, 76, 78–79, 81, 91, 100, 115, 144
Development and General Purpose Committee (D&GPC), 65, 75–76

Education Commission (EC), x, 67, 69, 82, 87, 119–24, 127–28, 131–34, 136–37, 139, 146
Education Commission Report No. 6 (ECR-6), x, 67, 121, 124, 128–29, 137, 139
Education Commission Report No. 7 (ECR-7), x, 67, 121, 124, 131–32, 137, 139
Ellison, Mary, 36
Endocrinology and Metabolic Diseases Unit (Division), 54–55, 116, 139
Executive Council, 85, 122, 109
Extradition Bill of 2019, 88

Faculty of Medicine or Medical Faculty, xii, xiii, 16, 28, 30, 36, 46, 71–72, 76–80, 92, 93, 138
'Fit for Purpose' report, 65, 89

INDEX

Fong, C. P. (Chun Piu), 44, 142
Fong, C. P. Gold Medal, 40
Fulton, J. S., 55

General Purpose Committee (GPC), 65
General Teaching Council, 132
Gibson, James, 79
Glasgow Royal Infirmary, 49
Gold Bauhinia Star (GBS), 140, 143
government hospital(s), 108–9, 111
Grand Bauhinia Medal (GBM), 140, 143

HKU iGift-Rosie Young Scarf program, 71
HKU Student Union, 88–89
Halnan, Keith E., 94
Han, Suyin, 38, 39, 83
Harcourt, C. H. J., 26
Ho, Ko Tsun, 14
Holmes, Ronald, 96
Hong Kong Academy of Medicine (Academy of Medicine), 64, 95, 143–45
Hong Kong College of Medicine, 4, 14, 16
Hong Kong College of Physicians (HKCP), 63–64, 95, 140, 143–44, 146
Hong Kong Council of Early Childhood Education and Services (CECES), 123–24
Hong Kong Examination Authority (Examinations and Assessment Authority), 119, 146
Hong Kong Medical Association, 98, 101
Hong Kong Medical Council (Medical Council), x–xi, 66, 69, 77, 90, 93–100, 99n20, 114, 116, 122, 139, 145–46
Hong Kong University Council (University Council), xii, 69, 88, 90, 147
Hong Kong University Faculty of Dentistry, 91, 116

Hong Kong University Foundation for Educational Development and Research (HKU Foundation), 69, 71, 85, 90, 92, 145
Hospital Authority (HA), x, 102, 107, 109–13, 116–17, 139, 145
Hou, Pao Chang, 37–38, 39, 40, 142
Hsieh, Arnold, 66, 76–77
Huang, Chi-To, 38–39, 39
Huang, Rayson, ix, 65–66, 75–76, 81–85, 88
hypoglycaemia, 56, 70

Jiangxi Medical School, 22, 39, 44

Kempeitai, 21
King, Gordon, 36–38
Kuomintang (KMT), 6, 10, 17, 19, 30
Kwong Wah Middle School, 24–25

Lady Ho Tung Hall, 36–37
Lam, Carrie, *103*, 103, 107
Language Fund Advisory Committee, 87, 129, 146
Lee, Quo Wei, 120, 122
Legislative Council, 80, 82, 97, 99, 109, 129
Leung, Antony K. C., 133
Leung, Michael Man-kin, 122, 124
Licentiate Committee of the Medical Council, 66, 93, 95, 97, 145
Lofts, Brian, 81

MacLehose, Murray, 64, 82
McFadzean, A. J. S. (Old Mac), 39–40, 42, 42–43, 44, 46–47, 49, 53–55, 57–59, 60, *61*, 62, *63*, 65–66, 83, 118, 142
Medical and Health Department, x, xii, 44, 51–52, 60, 80, 108–9
Medical Clinic Ordinance 1963 (Cap 343), 96
Medical Registration (Amendment) Bill 1995, x, 95, 97

Medical Registration (Amendment) (No. 2) Bill 1995, 99
Medical Registration Ordinance, Chapter 161, 93
Medical Registration (Transitional Provisions) Bill 1997, 97
medium of instruction (MOI), 120, 124, 126–27, 129–30
Member of the Order of the British Empire (MBE), 34
Monitoring Committee on Implementation of the SARS Expert Committee Report's Recommendations, 69, 146
Morris, Paul, 121–22
Most Excellent Order of the British Empire (OBE), 140, *141*, 143

Needham, Joseph, 37, 55–56
Northcote Science Building, 28, 31, 32

Occupy Central Movement, 88, 88n28
Official Languages Ordinance, 125
On Lan Street, 12, 20
Open Learning Institute of Hong Kong (Open University of Hong Kong, Hong Kong Metropolitan University), 135–36, 140, 143
Organisation for Economic Co-operation and Development (OECD), x, 67, 120

Patten, Chris, 123
Peking Union Medical College (PUMC), 38, 42, 78
People's Republic of China, 17, 30, 78, 83, 94, 130
periodic paralysis, 56–57, 70
pre-primary education, 121, 124
primary health care, x, xiii, 100–102, 104–5, 107, 116, 139, 145
Primary Healthcare Authority, 107

Primary Healthcare Blueprint Symposium—Reform on the Road, 107
Prince of Wales Hospital, 81, 114
Princess Margaret Hospital, 115–16, 146
Prince Philip Dental Hospital, 115, 145
Pro-Vice-Chancellor, ix–x, xiii, 67, 76, 80–84, 86–88, 91–92, 102, 131, 135, 138, 145
Provisional Hospital Authority (PHA), x, 107, 109–12, 139, 145

QS World University Rankings, 116
Queen Mary Hospital, 37, 40, *41*, 44–45, 49, 52–55, 60, 66, 71, 80, 116, 139, 144
Queen's College (Central School, Victoria College), 7–8, 16

Ride, Lindsay, 32–34, *33*
Rosie Young 90 Medal for Outstanding Young Woman Scholar, 71
Royal College of Physicians of Edinburgh, 49, 140, 147
Royal College of Physicians of London, 49, 140

SARS Expert Committee, 69, 113–14, 117, 139, 146
SARS Expert Committee Report, 114
Sacred Heart School (Sacred Heart Canossian College), 15, 24, 27–28
school-based management (SBM), 82, 130–32, 137
school management initiative (SMI), 131, 133
Scott, W. D., 109
Secretary for the Education and Manpower, 122, 124
Secretary for Health and Welfare, 99
Senior Management Team, 65, 138
Senior Pro-Vice-Chancellor, 87, 145

severe acute respiratory syndrome
   (SARS), 69, 112–15
Shiqi (Shekki), 3–4, 7–8, 11
sishu, 6–7
Sino-British Joint Declaration, 65, 82, 94, 126
Sino-British Trust Scholarship, 47
Siu, Shui Ying, 6, *10*
Standing Committee on Language Education and Research (SCOLAR), 129
Sub-dean of the Faculty of Medicine, ix–x, xiii, 66, 76–77, 79–80, 91, 93, 144
subvented hospital(s), 102, 108–11
Sun, Yat-sen, 4–5, 10, 15, 17
swine flu, 114–15
Szeto, Wah, 86, 129

Tai, Benny, 88
Tai Yuk Primary School, 14–15
The Chinese University of Hong Kong (CUHK), 44, 80–81, 88n28, 114, 122, 125
The University of Hong Kong, vi, viii, ix–xii, xiii, xiv, 8, 8n9, 9, 16, 22, 28, 29, 30–31, 33–40, 49, 52, 59, 62, 65–67, 69, 71–72, 75–92, 93, 96, 100, 102, 104, 114–16, 118, 122–24, 131, 134–36, 138–40, 143–46
thyrotoxicosis, 50, 56–57, 70
Tiananmen Square incident, 68, 86–87
Todd, David, 58, 61–62, 63, 64, 78, 84, 95
Tse, Tsan-tai, 15
Tung Wah Hospital, 16, 20

United States National Institute of Health (NIH), 58, 147
University Grants Committee (Hong Kong), 91, 146
University of California at San Francisco (UCSF), 57, 145

University of Michigan, 57–58
University Medical Unit (UMU), 40, 42, 44–45, 52, 54–55, 60
Umbrella Movement, 88

Visiting Team for the Review of Education and Training in the University of Hong Kong and the Chinese University of Hong Kong, 114, 146

Wang, Christina, 55
Wang, Gungwu, ix, 84–88, 122
White Paper on Development of Medical Services in Hong Kong, 51
White Paper on Development of Senior Secondary and Tertiary Education, 1978, 119
White Paper on Secondary Education over the Next Decade, 1974, 119, 126
Woo, Peter, 112
Working Party on Postgraduate Medical Education and Training, 64, 93–94, 145
Working Party on Unregistrable Doctors, 96
Working Party on Primary Health Care (WPPHC), x, 100–107, *103*, 116–17, 139, 145
Working Party on Primary Health Care (WPPHC) Report, 105

xiucai, 5, 5n5, 7

Yeung, Ho Lam, 11, 22
Yeung, Sau Han (Rosie), 11, 14
Yeung, Sau Man (Pauline), 11, 15, 22
Yeung, Shun Hang, 5–8, 8n9, *9–10*, 11, 16, 22
Yeung, Tse Tse, ix, 14–15
Yeung, Wai Lam, 11, 15–16, 20, 22–23, 30, 47, 60

Yeung, Woon Lam, 11, 16–17, 22–24, 30, 39, 44, 60
Young, Frank, 55
Young, Mark, 20
Young, Kenneth Leonard, 81, 86